MYTHS
AND
LEGENDS
FROM AROUND THE WORLD

A Marshall Edition

This book was conceived, edited, and designed by
Marshall Editions, 170 Piccadilly, London W1V 9DD

Executive Editor: Cynthia O'Brien
Managing Editor: Kate Phelps
Project Editor: Kate Scarborough
Art Director: Branka Surla
Design Manager: Ralph Pitchford
Editorial Director: Ruth Binney
Production: Barry Baker, Janice Storr
Research: Jazz Wilson, Liz Ferguson

Published by Evans Brothers Ltd, 2A Portman Mansions,
Chiltern Street, London W1M 1LE

ISBN 0 237 51488 5

Originated by Fotographics UK/Hong Kong
Printed and bound in Italy by Officine Grafiche De
Agostini–Novara

British Library Cataloguing-in-Publication data available
on request from the British Library.

MYTHS
— AND —
LEGENDS
FROM AROUND THE WORLD

by Sandy Shepherd
Illustrated by Tudor Humphries

EVANS BROTHERS LIMITED

Contents

Inside a temple in India people watch a dancer acting out a Hindu myth. This is one of the ways stories have been passed down the generations.

Introduction

Everyone asks, at some time, "How did the world begin?" And when floods, earthquakes or lightning strike, people look for an answer to the question "Why?" But it isn't only occasional disasters that make us wonder. The world is so well ordered, it seems to run like clockwork. It is amazing that the sun rises every day; that the moon waxes and wanes every 28 days; that summer and winter, rainy seasons and dry seasons happen at the same time each year. To explain these events people often told stories to each other. They also told stories as a way of remembering history—great battles, heroes and heroines and great leaders of the past. Over the years these stories have been written down and are called myths or legends.

Because there was less travel in the past, most people knew what life was like only in the place where they lived. Their myths describe their own world and they tell them in their own way. In each chapter there is a section on myths in daily life. These stories give an insight into the way people in the past lived.

Myths are poetic tales explaining why the world is the way it is and why people behave the way they do. They usually involve gods and goddesses, or spirits. Legends are stories about events that may or may not have taken place a long time ago. Both myths and legends may have formed part of a religious world and were woven into people's daily lives. They may seem fantastic and unbelievable, but this is part of the art of storytelling. Myths and legends are exciting, sad, magical—and they are always good stories.

This book is a collection of myths and legends from around the world. There are maps on pages 94 and 95 which show you where they originated.

The stories in this book can be read alone or, better still, read aloud, remembered and told again and again, just as they were in the past.

Narcissus flowers
(page 23)

THE WORLD WE LIVE IN

The many peoples on Earth live in different worlds. Some live in lands of snow and ice. Others live where it is always hot, where birds are brightly coloured and animals have strongly patterned skins and fur. Some people live on islands surrounded by water. Others live on great plains in the middle of vast landmasses where they never see the sea. In all of these places people tell stories about how their world came to be.

In many countries, such as Japan and New Zealand, people say that the land rose up from the water. In other countries, such as Egypt and Tahiti,

Thoth, the
Egyptian god
(page 16)

Ymir, the
ice giant
(page 16)

King Lion of
Russia
(page 23)

The creation of Tahiti
(pages 12-15)

The Guatemalan sky god sent down a storm (page 17)

The world on the back of a turtle (page 17)

A peacock's feather (pages 20-21)

the stories tell of how the world was born from an egg when it split into two. It does not matter whether these stories are believed or not. They are just one way of explaining the world.

Some of these stories are also about animals and plants. In Africa, children ask "How did the leopard get its spots?" And in India, there is a tale about how the peacock came to be such a beautiful bird.

Another question people often ask is "How were we created?" In Guatemala they once said that two gods made people from clay. In Scandinavia it was said that a giant cow licked an icy rock to free the first man.

A leopard from Sierra Leone (page 22)

A Maori house post depicting Rangi and Papa (pages 18-19)

The Heavenly Floating Bridge of Japan (pages 10-11)

Myths in Daily Life
The Birth of Japan

In an ancient Japanese book, called the *Nihongi*, there is an old myth about the creation of Japan. This book was written in Chinese because it was the Chinese who taught the Japanese how to write and part of this myth comes from China.

At first, the book says, the world was like the inside of an egg and had not quite formed. Slowly, the clear liquids rose to become the sky. The heavier bits sank to form a jelly-like Earth. Land floated across the jelly just like oil floats on water.

Then a reed grew out of the Earth and turned into two spirits. These spirits created seven pairs of gods called Kami. The last pair was Izanagi and his wife, Izanami.

The other Kami gods gave Izanagi and Izanami a spear—the Heavenly Jewelled Spear with a shaft made from coral. They ordered Izanagi and Izanami to finish creating the world with it. Izanagi and Izanami stood on a rainbow called the Heavenly Floating Bridge. They stirred the liquid beneath them with the tip of the spear and when they lifted it up, a drop of liquid fell from the spear and formed an island.

Izanagi and Izanami built a palace and a sacred pillar on the island. According to

Izanagi and Izanami stood on the Heavenly Floating Bridge. As the Heavenly Jewelled Spear was lifted, a drop of liquid fell from it and formed an island.

Japanese tradition, they walked around the pillar. Izanagi went one way. Izanami went the other. When they met on the other side, Izanami said to her husband, "How handsome you are." "How charming you are," said her husband. But he was unhappy, because the rule was that the husband should speak first to his wife, not the other way round. This rule is still observed by some people in Japan.

When Izanami had a baby, it turned out to be a baby leech. She put it on a reed in the water—where leeches live today—and left it. Izanagi and Izanami asked the gods why they did not have the kind of children they wanted. The gods told them that it was because Izanami had spoken to her husband first. So Izanagi and Izanami went back to the island and walked around the pillar again. This time Izanagi spoke first to his wife. When Izanami next had a baby she gave birth to eight islands, which grew into the land of Japan—a chain of islands in the Pacific Ocean.

After all their work, Izanagi and Izanami were hungry. So Izanagi created the god of rice to give them some food to eat. Rice is the most important food in Japan today.

The last child Izanami had was the god of fire but as he was born, he burned her so badly that she died. Now alone, Izanagi went to the river to wash his face. As he washed, the Sun was born out of his left eye and the Moon out of his right eye. And from his nose—where sneezes come from—the storm god was born. Izanagi had finished creating the world and was glad that Izanami had helped him create such a beautiful place.

Ta'aroa

*According to the Tahitians, the world was made
by Ta'aroa who escaped from his shell and used his body to
create land and animals.*

On the islands of Tahiti, in the south Pacific Ocean, storytellers speak of Ta'aroa. Before the world was formed, Ta'aroa lived in a floating egg. All around the egg there was nothing but darkness, silence and cold.

Ta'aroa grew tired of sitting in his egg. He started to push against the shell. He pushed and pushed until it cracked open into two halves. Then he climbed out, gave a big yawn and stretched out his arms. Ta'aroa looked around, but he could see nothing except darkness. He screwed up his eyes, trying to see something in the darkness. But he still saw nothing. He rubbed his eyes and opened them again. Still there was blackness and, what was more, Ta'aroa could hear nothing. He climbed on to the shell, put his hands to his mouth and called out, "Coo-ee!" His voice bounced back as it echoed in the silence. He waited, but no one replied.

Because he felt cold and lonely, Ta'aroa got back into the shell and pulled the other half over him. He sat there thinking what to do. Then he had an idea. If there was no world out there, he would make it himself! So he pushed open the shell again. He took one half and threw it up into the air. It stayed up there and became the sky. He pushed the other half downward and it became the Earth.

Looking up and down at his work, Ta'aroa was pleased. But something worried him. There was still nothing between the Earth and sky except himself. So he decided to use his body to make the rest of the world. He took his spine and ribs and flung them down on the Earth. The curved bones and ridged vertebrae turned into mountains. He took out his lungs, his heart, his liver and his kidneys and threw them up into the sky. There they turned into clouds of many different shapes.

Next Ta'aroa spread out his flesh and it became rich soil. His long, rippling intestines became the eels and shellfish in the sea. His shiny, pearly nails became the seashells and the scales on the fish. And from his blood he made everything that is red in the world: sunrise and sunset, the red in the rainbow and birds with red feathers.

But Ta'aroa was still not satisfied. There was still darkness in the world. This was because the sky god Atea was trapped on the

In darkness Ta'aroa broke out of his shell. He wanted to see what was around him. When he realized that all was black and still, he thought of a plan. He decided to create a world from the shell and his body. Light was the only thing he could not provide. This came from the god Atea.

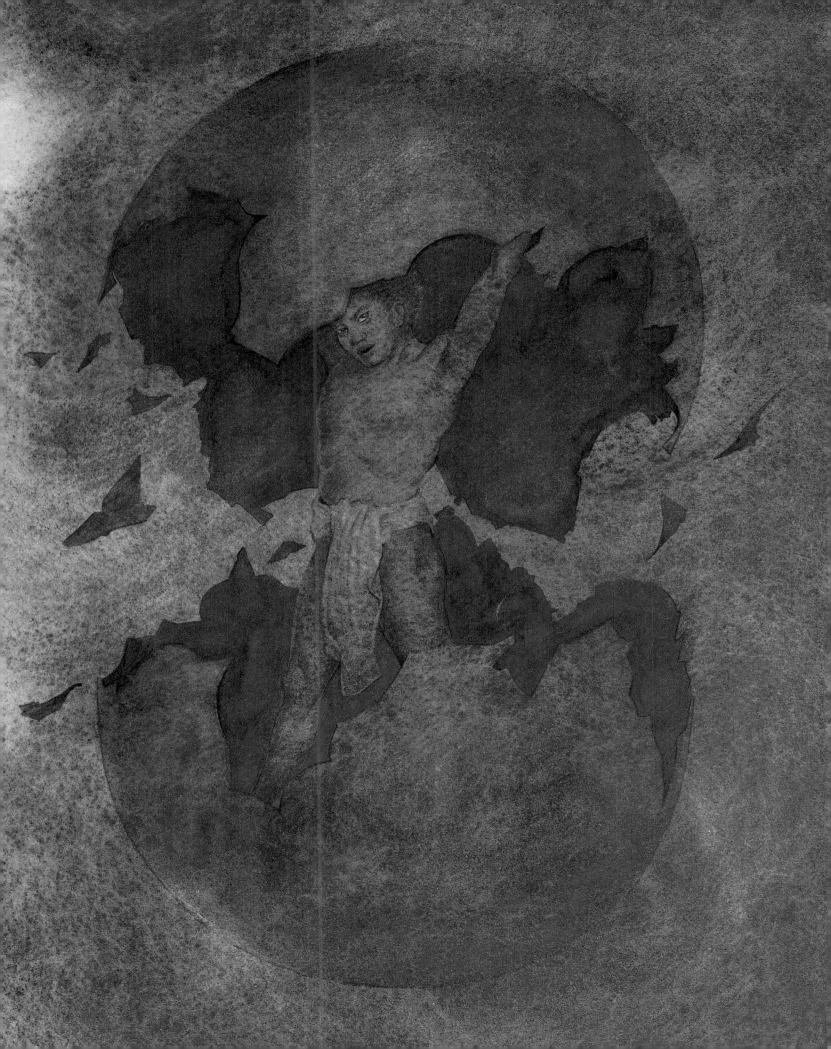

Earth by a giant octopus. The octopus had wrapped itself so tightly around the world that Atea could not rise into the sky to let light shine on it.

Ta'aroa could not fight the octopus himself. He had used up his body to create the world. Now he was just a spirit. But he still had a voice. He called out to the gods for help. One god, called Rua, cast a spell on the octopus, and killed it. But even though it was dead, its arms stayed clamped around the Earth.

Another god, Ru, pushed against the octopus with all his strength. He even managed to lift the octopus up a bit and let the sky god rise up off the Earth just a little. As he did this, another god, called Maui, quickly pushed great rocks and trees between Atea and the Earth. "Push again. Push harder, Ru," said Maui. But Ru could push no more. The effort was too great for him. His stomach burst and his intestines floated up to the sky and formed more clouds.

So Maui went to ask the great god Tane if he would help. Tane came down with a club and knocked holes into the octopus's tentacles and

chopped them off. One by one the tentacles let go of the Earth. They fell into the sea and turned into islands. Once the god Atea was freed, he shot up into the sky. And there was light in the world.

Now that the gods could see, they looked down at the Earth Ta'aroa had made. But they made a face at what they saw. Ta'aroa had been working in the dark, so he could not see what he was doing. Everything had a strange colour and a strange shape. So Tane put everything right and gave the world the colours and shape it has now. He made stars to brighten the night sky. He gave the fish many beautiful patterns and colours. And he made the shells the jewels of the ocean.

Once the world had been created, the gods started making people. Ta'aroa built a temple where people could worship him. The people wanted to make Ta'aroa happy, so that he would make their crops plentiful. They made sacrifices to Ta'aroa at his temple. But they grew forgetful, and after some time did not make sacrifices any more. Ta'aroa was angry and sent a great storm to Tahiti. The roaring sea rose so high that it flooded the land. Now the land he created pokes up above the water as many smaller islands.

Wielding a heavy club, the mighty god Tane rushed to defeat the giant octopus. By chopping off its tentacles, the sky god was released and finally light came to the world Ta'aroa had created.

Creating The World

Egypt

The ancient Egyptians believed that at the beginning of time the world was just a dark liquid called Nun. In Nun there was an egg, which held four gods and four goddesses. There was also Thoth, a god who looked like a bird called an ibis. The gods and goddesses were trapped in the egg. But when Thoth woke up from a deep sleep and started singing, the egg hatched and the gods and goddesses escaped. Then they made the world.

Scandinavia

In the myths of northern Europe, it is said that before the world was created there was just space. Then Niflheim, a world of clouds and shadows, formed in the north. And in it a fountain spurted cold water that turned into rivers of ice. In the south was Muspellheim, a land of fire. Warm air blew from this fiery region on to the icy north and started to melt it. The melting water created a sea, called Ginunngagap, and out of it was born a giant, whose name was Ymir.

The ice continued to melt, and a cow was created out of it. The cow liked salt, so she licked the salt off the icy rocks. One day, as she licked a rock, a hair appeared. After three days of licking, a man emerged. His name was Buri. Buri's grandchildren became gods. They did not like Ymir and killed him. When he died, his head became the sky and his flesh became the land. And so the world began.

North America

The Onondaga of North America say that in the beginning there was no Earth. There was Skyland, where a

chief and his people lived. And below was water with animals swimming in it. One night the chief's youngest wife dreamed that a big tree had been uprooted. According to Onondaga tradition, everything must be done to make an important dream come true. So, the next morning, the chief and his son uprooted the tree. Where its roots had been, there was a big hole. The chief's wife looked in and saw water shining far beneath. She leaned closer and fell through the hole.

The animals in the water saw the woman falling towards them. Two swans spread their wings to catch her. Muskrat dived far beneath the water to bring back some soil for the woman to stand on. The animals put the soil on the back of a giant turtle and it began to grow. The soil grew until it became the world, then the woman stood on the soil. Some seeds that were in her hand fell on to the soil and started growing into plants. The creation of the Earth had begun.

Guatemala

Mayans of Guatemala used to say that, at the beginning of time, there was the sky and the sea. Land lay far beneath the sea. The god Gucamatz asked the sky god Hurakan if he could make the sea part and the land rise up. Then they could create people who would worship them. Hurakan agreed. He sent down lightning and thunder and the sea parted. The Earth lifted up, mountains rose into the sky and trees sprouted on the land. Gucamatz made animals. But the animals could not talk, so the gods took some clay and made people, who could sing their praises.

Rangi and Papa

Papa, the Earth goddess, and Rangi, the sky god, were so much in love that they would not let go of each other. Light came to the world only when they were separated.

In the stories told by the Maori of New Zealand, the Earth goddess is called Papa, and her husband is Rangi, the sky god. When the world was created, Rangi and Papa were so much in love that they hugged each other and would not let go. This meant that the Earth and the sky were always joined, and no light could come into the world.

Papa gave birth to several children, but they were stuck between their parents and could not escape. Finally the children decided that they had to get out. One of them, Tane, suggested that they force their parents apart. The children agreed. One by one they tried, without success. Then Tane had a try. He folded himself up very small and slipped between his parents. With his feet against Rangi and his shoulders against Papa, he pushed. He pushed for hours, which ran into days and then into weeks. He pushed for years and years. And very slowly Tane managed to uncurl his body, straighten himself and finally push his parents apart.

Light came into the world. And for the first time since it was created, plants started to grow. But Rangi and Papa were so sad to be apart that they cried and cried. Rangi's tears ran into rivers. They became a sea. They even threatened to flood the whole world. Something had to be done. One of the children turned Papa over so that Rangi could not see her face. Now he doesn't cry so much. But you can still see his tears every morning—they are the dewdrops on the grass. And the mists that rise from the ground are Papa's sighs.

The sky god Rangi cried so much when he was separated from his wife, the Earth goddess Papa, that he caused terrible floods. The only way to stop him was to turn Papa over so that he could not see her.

Indra and the Peacock

*In ancient India people told the story of
how the peacock came to be so much more
beautiful than the peahen.*

There was a time, long ago, when peacocks were very plain birds. You could hardly tell them from the female peahens. Both were brown, with long tails and ugly wrinkled feet. And both had a terrible cry. It was so loud and harsh that it sounded as if someone had just grabbed the bird by the throat.

One day, a peacock was busily pecking at insects on the ground when the sky god, Indra, rushed past. The peacock called out,

"What are you running away from?" Indra answered, breathlessly, that the demon king Ravana was chasing him. Now, even though Indra was a god and lightning was his weapon, nothing could hurt Ravana. The only thing Indra could do to save himself was to run away.

Just then, the peacock and Indra heard Ravana's heavy giant feet thundering towards them. Quickly, the peacock spread his tail and Indra crouched

down behind him. The demon ran past without a sideways glance, into the jungle. A sigh of relief came from behind the peacock. "Thank you," said Indra. "Such a brave bird should not be so plain. I will make you the most beautiful bird in the world." He bowed to the peacock, and as he did, the peacock's brown feathers turned a brilliant blue, and his tail became a fabulous green with a thousand golden eyes.

The peacock became very proud and very vain. He strutted about, making sure everyone looked at him. Every time he saw a peahen, he opened his magnificent tail to show her how beautiful he was. But he was not completely beautiful. Whenever the peacock looked down at his ugly feet, he gave a loud cry of horror. And his tail sank and closed up as he became humble again.

In ancient India, people said that the peacock's cry was a sign that a storm was about to break. Indra, the bringer of rain, had made the peacock his herald.

The peacock was made beautiful because he did a good deed for the god Indra. He hid Indra from the demon god Ravana. Indra was so pleased that he changed the peacock from a dull brown bird to the fabulous bird it is today.

Plants and Animals

Canada

The Inuit tell a story of a man and his son travelling through the icy Arctic wastes, gathering food and fuel for winter. The boy made friends with a little brown bird. When winter set in, the boy and his father settled into their igloo. One night they heard a polar bear outside. The bear tried to get into the igloo, but was too big. So he put his paw through the entrance and stamped out the fire inside. The bear knew that, in the spring, he could come and get the boy and his father, who would have frozen to death. Once the bear had gone the little bird flew into the igloo. The bird saw that the boy and his father were so cold that they had fallen asleep and frantically flapped his wings to get the fire going again. As he flapped, the flames grew, and the bird's breast turned red with the heat. He did not stop until the boy and his father had woken. Since then, robins have had a red breast.

Sierra Leone

At one time Leopard, a big sand-coloured cat, was friends with Fire and used to go to see Fire often. But Fire never came to Leopard's house. Leopard asked Fire why he never came to visit him. Fire said that he never left his house. But Leopard begged and begged. Finally Fire said, "If you make a path of dry leaves from my house to yours, then I'll come." So Leopard and his wife gathered an armful each of dry leaves and scattered them on the ground all the way from Fire's house to their house. They then closed the door.

Soon they heard a crackling sound outside. "Ah! Fire is here," said Leopard, and he opened the door. Fire's fingers touched Leopard and they were so hot that Leopard and his wife had to jump out of the window to get away. Now leopards have dark spots on their fur where Leopard was burned by Fire.

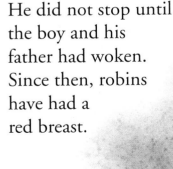

Russia

A Russian myth tells of how, in the beginning, the only animal to have a tail was King Lion. One by one, animals came to him to ask for a tail like his. King Lion called his wizards and told them to make him tails. Eventually the tails were made and brought to King Lion in a casket.

He sent the birds out to tell all the animals to come and get their tails. The first animal to reach the palace was the fox, who took the most handsome, thickest tail. The horse chose a long tail. The squirrel took a fluffy tail. The last in the queue was the rabbit. All that was left in the casket was a scrap of fur.

When all the tails had gone, the bear arrived. He had been asleep when the birds came with their message. He saw the badger admiring his new striped tail. The bear wanted it, but the badger started to run away. The bear put his great paw on the badger's tail and caught a piece of fluff. He used this for a tail—and even now the bear's tail is so small that you can hardly see it.

Greece

The young Greek man Narcissus was so handsome that many people fell in love with him. But he turned them all away. He could love no one but himself. The nymph Echo fell in love with him, but Narcissus just pretended she was not there. In her grief, Echo wasted away until all that was left of her was her voice—an echo.

The goddess Nemesis, who thought Narcissus very vain, was sorry for Echo. She cast a spell on Narcissus, making him look at himself in a pool of water for the rest of his life. The more Narcissus looked at his reflection, the more he fell in love with himself. Every day he lay at the pool's edge staring at his beautiful face. He would not eat or sleep. He grew thinner and eventually died. The gods turned him into a flower called a narcissus. The pretty flower grows happily at the water's edge, and its head hangs as if it is looking at itself.

THE HEAVENS AND THE EARTH

The Japanese sun goddess, Amaterasu (page 33)

The heavens, or the skies, are full of fascinating things. In most parts of the world the sun rises and sets every day. But in the polar regions the sun rises for only six months of the year—and then it is so bright that it does not seem to set. In the night sky, the moon grows full every 28 days and then shrinks. The stars appear in patterns, or constellations. And then there are eclipses, when the sun or the moon vanishes from the sky for a short time.

Beneath the sky, the Earth is just as full of surprising events. Floods drown parts of it. Lightning strikes it and sets trees on fire. Some plants appear above the ground in spring, and wither in autumn and winter. Volcanoes explode with fiery lava

Zeus, the most powerful of the Greek gods (pages 40-41)

The African King Yam,
home of the yam spirit
(pages 26-27)

The Chinese
Divine Archer
(pages 28-31)

and earthquakes rock the ground until it cracks open.
Today we have scientific explanations for all these
events. But in the past, and even now in some parts of
the world, gods and spirits were thought to be
responsible for these fantastic happenings. The stories
told about them are much more imaginative
than the scientific explanations.

There is the Chinese myth about why there is
only one sun in the sky. In Indonesia there is a
tale that a giant pig scratching its back causes
an earthquake. The seasons are explained in
Greek mythology with the story of Persephone and
Hades. These are just some of the myths about natural
events from around the world.

Mount Etna,
on the island
of Sicily
(pages 40-41)

Hades, the Greek god of the
underworld, and
Persephone (page 38)

Myths in Daily Life
Ale, the Ibo Earth Goddess

The Ibo people form one of the many tribes in Nigeria, Africa. They live mainly in the southeastern part of the country. Some live in towns with cars and three-storey houses, but many others still live in villages deep within the thick forests of oil palms and creepers.

Their mud houses with thatched roofs line dusty paths that wind through the trees. Near the houses are gardens where the women grow most of the food that the Ibo eat— corn, melons, pumpkins and beans. But the most important food, which the men grow, is yams. To make sure that this vegetable grows each year, the traditional Ibo people pray to their Earth goddess, Ale. They believe that she makes the crops grow and protects the harvest. She also gives birth to people. And when they die, she takes them back into her womb and down to the underworld.

The Ibo pray to Ale every year when they plant their yams. They plant them in February so that they are ready for the rains, which come in April. The men plant the tubers in mounds of soil that look like little hills and around the mounds they place clay figures that are painted red and blue. These Ale dolls make the yams grow well.

When the yams are ready to be dug up, there is a celebration. A big feast is laid out and sometimes an animal is sacrificed. Music is played with bamboo rattles, flutes, bells and drums, and everyone dances. But no one is allowed to eat any of the new yams. They have to be stored a little while before the yam priest decides that they are ready to be eaten. The Ibo believe that if they break this rule no one will be able to have a baby and no more crops will grow. It is actually wise to leave the young yams because they are poisonous. They are only safe to eat when they are ripe.

Every year at harvest time a new shrine is built for Ale. These shrines are named Mbari houses. The yam priest decides when to build the shrine. This is usually after he has received some sort of sign. This could be a snake suddenly appearing in his garden. Then he chooses the men and women who will help him to build the Mbari house.

The shrines are square houses with verandas around them. The pillars around and inside the shrines are painted with patterns, and colourful cloths are hung inside. The shrines are also filled with brightly painted clay figures with Ale always in the middle. She often has a child on her

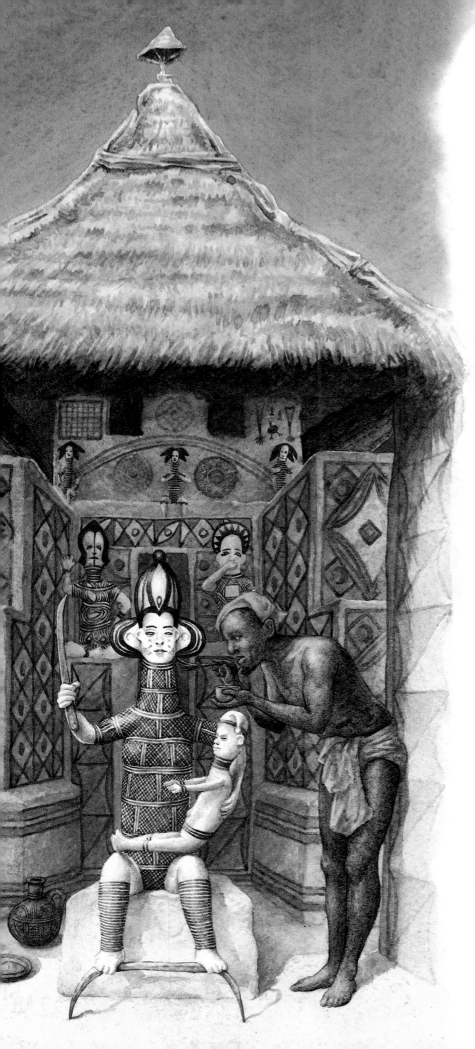

knees because she is the goddess that brings children into the world. She also has rings painted on her legs, like the brass rings that Ibo girls wear. The girls put them on when they are ready to have children. Near her is a figure of the storm god, her brother. When the storms threaten the skies, the Ibo beat the drums for this god. A figure of the water goddess, Ale's sister, is also placed in the shrine.

When the yams are dug up, the Ibo priest keeps aside the biggest one. This is called the King Yam and the yam spirit lives in it. Chicken's or goat's blood is poured over it to keep the yam spirit happy and the grateful spirit protects the crop from being stolen or harmed.

When the yams are ripe, the women take them to market. They usually also take palm oil, which they make from crushing the kernels of palm nuts. At market, the women bargain for the right price with the people who buy yams. Just before the women leave for market, their children may say to them, "Mother, gain from the market people: market people, lose to mother."

A shrine to the Earth goddess Ale is being painted by a member of the Ibo tribe. The Ibo name these shrines Mbari houses. They build them at harvest time as thanks to Ale for their crop of yams. The Ibo priest chooses the people who are going to help build and decorate the shrine. It is a great honour to do this job. Those chosen work hard to make it pleasing to the goddess Ale.

The Divine Archer

*According to the Chinese, there was once a time
when the world had ten suns. This story explains
why there is only one left in the sky.*

In Chinese mythology, the god of the eastern sky, Di Jun, and his wife, Xi He, had ten sons. The family lived in the east, in the branches of a giant tree that was thousands of metres tall. This tree was on the other side of the sea.

Every day, while it was still dark, Xi He would wake up one of her boys. They would both climb into her chariot, which was pulled by a dragon, and she would take him to a place in the sky to begin his work. The boy's job was to walk across the sky. You see, her children were suns. And the eastern sky where they lived is where the sun rises.

After a thousand years of doing this every day, the boys grew bored. They decided it

would be far more interesting if they went to work together. So early one morning the ten boys got up quietly, trying very hard not to wake their mother, and all ten started to walk across the sky.

As the morning wore on, the heat from the ten suns became fiercer and fiercer. The sky grew whiter and whiter. The Earth grew hotter and hotter and plants started to shrivel up and die. Rivers and lakes began to run dry, while the ground was baked hard and started to crack. It was so hot that animals and people grew weak with thirst, hunger, heat and exhaustion.

The emperor Shun pleaded with the boys' father, Di Jun, "Please make them go back," he said. "The Earth will die if you do not stop your sons." Di Jun called to his sons and

The Chinese goddess Xi He drove a chariot, which was pulled by a dragon. Every day she took one of her ten sons to the place where he started his journey across the sky. By doing this, she made sure that the Earth got the right amount of sun each day.

The Divine Archer, Hou I, shot at the ten suns to save the world from shrivelling up under the heat and dying. He had ten arrows, one for each sun. However, the emperor realized that the world needed a sun, so he sent a messenger to remove one arrow. In that way he saved one sun, which would rise in the east and set in the west every day.

told them to stop and go back home, but they would not listen. Instead they climbed higher and higher to the middle of the sky.

The other gods in the sky were looking down and watching. They felt sorry for the people on Earth. "Di Jun, you must do something," they said. So Di Jun thought about the problem, but the only answer he could think of was a very sad one. He went to see the Divine Archer, Hou I, who lived in the sky. Di Jun gave him a magic bow and arrows and told him to shoot down the suns.

Hou I had once been an ordinary man but he was such a good archer that he hit everything at which he aimed. The emperor had been so impressed that he had made him a god and named him the Divine Archer. Now he flew on the wind and lived only on the nectar of flowers.

Hou I flew down to the Earth on the wind. From there he could take good aim at the suns. He pulled back his bowstring and one by one he let his magic arrows fly. As each arrow hit a sun, the sun exploded with a huge flash of light. The boy inside it turned into a crow and plummeted headlong down to the Earth with an arrow through his breast.

The emperor was watching this and was very pleased. But, as each boy fell to the ground, a thought occurred to him. If Hou I shot down all the suns then the Earth would have no light or heat at all. So he called one of his courtiers and told him to run as fast as he could to Hou I and take one arrow out of his quiver. The courtier ran faster then he had ever run before. He got to Hou I just in time. Swiftly he plucked one arrow out. And so, today there is only one sun in the sky.

The Sun, the Moon and the Stars

Africa

Unkulunkulu, the Zulu's chief god, was also a sky god. Apart from bringing storms to the sky, the space in the sky was his. When people died he placed them in his heavens. You can see them at night—the Zulus believe that the stars are the dead people's eyes shining brightly in the sky.

Mexico

The Aztecs used to tell a story of their sun goddess. The world used to have four suns, but they all died. Now the Earth was dark. The gods met and agreed to make a sun and a moon. Two gods had to sacrifice themselves to become the sun and the moon. Tecciztecatl stepped forward. He was very vain and wanted to be the brightest thing in the sky. The gods picked the humblest goddess, Nanahuatzin, to be the moon. She was a leper, and they told her that if she agreed to be the moon, they would heal her skin and make her beautiful. The fires were lit. The gods ordered Tecciztecatl to jump in. Three times he pulled back because he was afraid. So the gods told Nanahuatzin to jump, and she did.

Tecciztecatl, worried that he would not be the sun after all, jumped in, too, but to the side of the fire where there were plenty of ashes. Just then, an eagle swooped into the flames and carried from them a beautiful ball of fire. It was Nanahuatzin. She had turned into the sun. Then a hawk flew into the fire and lifted out Tecciztecatl. He had become the moon.

Japan

The Japanese sun goddess Amaterasu had a brother, the storm god Susanowoo, who was always up to some mischief. One day he was so bad that he frightened Amaterasu and she hid inside a cave. With no sun, the world grew dark. The other gods begged her to come out, but she refused. So they decided to trick her. They put a mirror outside the cave. Then the goddess Uzume started making the other gods laugh. Inside the cave, Amaterasu wondered why they were laughing and came out of the cave. She was so startled to see her bright reflection that she just stood looking at it. Quickly, the other gods blocked the entrance to the cave with a stone. So Amaterasu made the world bright again.

North America

In the sky there is a pattern of stars called the Great Bear, or Ursa Major. A Micmac story tells how, in late spring, the bear wakes from its long sleep. It is chased by seven hunters disguised as stars. In summer they chase it across the northern horizon. In autumn, there are only three hunters left. They shoot their arrows and hit the bear. The bear rears up on its hind feet and eventually falls on its back. Its blood drips down to Earth and paints the leaves red. In winter, the skeleton of the bear lies on its back in the sky. But the bear's spirit enters another bear. The next spring, this other bear sets off across the sky.

Matsya

The Hindu Indians tell a tale of how the Earth was destroyed by a flood. Only one man, Manu, was warned by Matsya, the fish. Manu and his descendants are the ancestors of all Hindus.

A long time ago there was a wise Indian man named Manu. His name meant "father of mankind", and that is what he became.

One morning, Manu was washing his face in the river. He gathered the cool water in his hands and threw it against his face. It was good and made him feel fresh and ready to start the day. As he raised the water once more to his face, he saw a tiny fish in his cupped hands. "Save me, Manu," cried the fish. "I am so small, and the big fish eat little fish. I won't survive in the river."

Manu was very surprised to hear the fish talking. There was obviously something magical about it. So he did as the fish asked. He took the earthenware pot that was beside him, dipped it into the river, and put the fish into the pot. Very quickly, the fish started growing and was soon too big for the pot. So Manu put it into a tank. But it carried on growing. When it became too big for the tank, Manu put the fish into a lake. But soon even the lake was too small for it. Manu took the fish down to the sea and let it go.

Before the fish swam off, it told Manu that

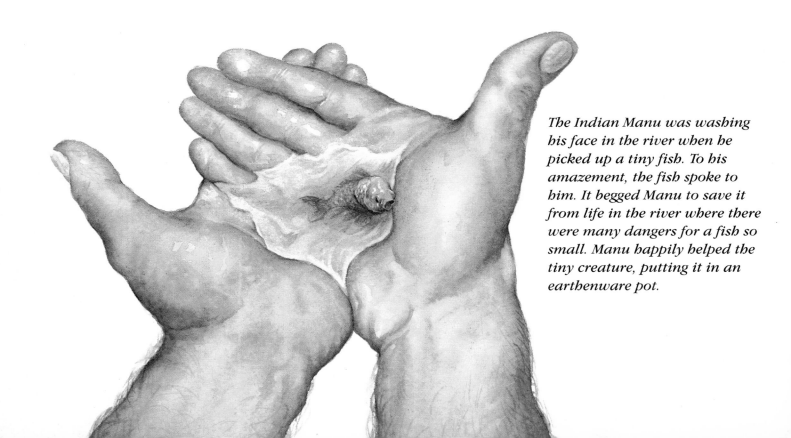

The Indian Manu was washing his face in the river when he picked up a tiny fish. To his amazement, the fish spoke to him. It begged Manu to save it from life in the river where there were many dangers for a fish so small. Manu happily helped the tiny creature, putting it in an earthenware pot.

darker and darker. Lightning flashed across the black sky. The heavens clapped and roared with thunder, like great drums being beaten. Then the rain began to fall. The drops were small at first, and pitter-pattered on the ground. But they grew larger and heavier and fell more and more quickly, until they made great craters in the mud. Manu rushed the last animals into the boat with the seven wise men, as the waters began to rise.

The waters lifted the boat off the ground and soon it was afloat. They drifted for a while, watching the houses, the trees, and then the hills slowly disappear beneath the water. Manu was getting a little worried. He did not know which direction to go in. Just then they felt a bump against the boat. Manu looked out of the porthole and saw his friend Matsya, the fish. It had grown even larger, and now had golden scales and a horn on its

its name was Matsya. The fish also told him that in a year's time there would be a great flood. To save himself, Manu should build a boat. And then he should get together seven wise men, like himself, as well as every plant seed and two of every kind of animal he could find. Matsya, the fish, would come and help them when the time came.

By now, Manu knew that this fish was very special, and it was probably telling the truth. So he did what the fish told him to do. First, he drew up a plan of a boat to see how much wood he would need. Then he cut down some trees and sawed them up for timber. With a hammer and nails, he fixed the wooden planks together until he had built a big boat. Then he started to look for the wise men, plants and animals.

It took him a year to complete his task. As he was gathering the last plants and loading them into his boat, he could see the storm clouds gathering. The sky grew

Matsya rapidly grew out of its earthenware pot so Manu put it into a tank. Again it grew so big that it had to be released into a lake. Even then the fish would not stop growing. Manu decided that the only place for it to live would be the sea. Before the fish left Manu, it warned him of the flood that was coming.

head. "Make a loop in your rope," said the fish, "and throw it over my horn." Manu did this, and the fish swam forward, towing the boat through the flood. When Manu and the wise men looked behind them, there was nothing left above the water. All they could see was the boat and the fish's horn ahead.

The flood lasted for years and years. And all this time the fish pulled them through the water. For years Manu and the wise men saw nothing else but themselves and the fish. Until, one day, they spotted some jagged rocks poking out of the water. The rocks were the mountain peaks of the Himalayas, the highest mountains in the world. "Throw your rope over that peak there," said Matsya. "Soon the waters will go down and your boat will float down with them."

Once again Manu did as the fish had told him. For a while the boat seemed to be floating in the same place. But everything was just as the fish said it would be. Slowly the rocks grew taller and taller as the boat went lower and lower. The men saw mountains appear and then hills, and soon the boat was touching the ground. Everyone cheered. They were so glad to see the ground again. Manu let out the animals, who were very relieved to be free again. They stretched their legs and necks. Some kicked out their back legs for joy. It had been a long time since they were able to prance about.

Manu and the wise men planted the seeds and started building homes. The crops soon flourished. The animals had settled in and had started to produce young. Manu and the wise men began writing down holy scriptures. But Manu was lonely. He called to the fish and said, "Please give me a wife. I need a companion." The fish answered, "I will give you a wife if you pray to me, for I am in fact a god, who has saved you."

Manu and the wise men built a temple to Matsya. Then they sacrificed a goat to keep Matsya happy. The fish then created a lovely wife for Manu and he was very happy. Manu and his wife had many children, who became ancestors of the Hindus.

Manu followed the fish's advice and built a boat. He gathered seven wise men and all the plants and animals he could find so that when the flood waters went down they could all start again. Matsya guided them during the flood and led them to safety on the Himalayan mountains.

The Forces of Nature

Hawaii

The Hawaiians once believed in a fire goddess called Pele, who lived in the crater of a volcano. She was usually quiet. But when she got angry, she poured molten lava from her head and turned people and animals into stone. Hawaii is a group of islands with many volcanoes that often erupt, sending boiling hot lava down their slopes. Any living thing that the lava flows over is turned rock hard when the lava cools and becomes solid.

Scandinavia

Thor was the thunder god of Norse myths. He was tall with red hair and rode a chariot pulled by two billy-goats. Pots hung on the sides of the chariot and, as Thor raced across the sky, they clattered, making the sound of thunder. One time Thor fought with a giant. He threw his hammer, called Mjollnir the Destroyer, at the giant. The giant hurled a great stone back. As the stone hit the hammer it smashed into little pieces. One piece hit the giant and killed him. Another flew into Thor's head and stayed there. Whenever this stone flashed, lightning struck the land.

Greece

The ancient Greeks believed that at one time summer was the only season. This changed when Persephone was kidnapped by the god of the underworld, Hades. He took her to his home underground. Persephone's mother, Demeter, the corn goddess, wandered around the world, crying. While she wandered, the plants withered and rivers and streams ran dry. The god Zeus begged Demeter to take care of the Earth once more. But Demeter refused unless she could see her daughter

again. Zeus told Hades to set Persephone free. Before Hades did this, he made Persephone eat some pomegranate seeds. This meant that Persephone was forced to return to him time and time again. So when Persephone is above ground, Demeter allows plants to grow. But six months later, when Persephone is underground, Demeter lets the plants die and the world is plunged into winter.

Central America

The Mayan moon goddess, Ix Chel, was also the Rainbow Lady. Because the moon affects the tides on Earth, it is associated with water. And so was Ix Chel. Her good side could be seen when she created rainbows, but her bad side appeared when she made floods. Ix Chel had a jug of water which she turned upside down. This jug was bottomless and the water spilled out, flooding the Earth and threatening to destroy it.

Indonesia

On the Indonesian island of Sulawesi there is a myth about earthquakes. The islanders say that the world is balanced on the back of a pig. When the pig's back becomes itchy it rubs against a giant palm tree. The world then rolls and shakes, as it does in an earthquake. The pig grunts with happiness as it scratches its back. These grunts are the loud rumbles that can be heard when there is an earthquake.

Typhon and Zeus

Volcanoes are one of nature's most spectacular sights, especially when erupting. This story explains how a volcano on the island of Sicily was formed.

Typhon was the son of the Earth goddess, Gaia. (He is also sometimes called Typhoeus.) He had a snake's tail and a hundred snake-like heads with flashing eyes and black tongues. Each head had a terrible voice. One boomed with the voice of a roaring god. Another snarled and foamed like a rabid dog. One bellowed like an enraged bull and another had an ear-splitting whistle. Thick bristles covered Typhon's heads and faces and snakes sprouted from his thighs. His body was covered with dirty feathers. As if he did not look frightening enough, this monster was also as tall as a mountain. At the mere sight of Typhon, the gods fled.

When Typhon was a child, his mother told him how Zeus, the father of the gods, had fought against her other children. She filled Typhon with anger against Zeus. And as soon as he was fully grown, he fought Zeus. At first, Typhon was losing the battle. Zeus hurled his thunderbolts at Typhon and drove him on to a mountain in Syria. But there Typhon stood his ground. He grabbed Zeus's arms and wrenched away his weapon. Then he tore out the sinews in his arms and legs, so that he could not move. Zeus just lay helpless on the ground. Typhon dragged him to his cave. He told a monster, who was part woman, part snake, to hide the sinews under a bearskin and to guard Zeus carefully.

Soon afterwards, two gods came looking for Zeus. They saw him in the cave. While one distracted the monster and made her look the other way, the other found the sinews and put them back into Zeus's arms and legs. They then flew off with him in a winged chariot back to Mount Olympus, the home of the gods.

Zeus fetched more thunderbolts and started to take his revenge on Typhon, whom he chased to Italy. Then with a huge effort, he tore a piece of land off the tip of Italy and threw it at Typhon. It landed on the monster and crushed him. The land became the island of Sicily.

Because the monster was immortal, he could not die, but was kept a prisoner under Sicily, in the depths of Mount Etna, the volcano. His jailer was the smith god, Hephaestus. Typhon could not escape because Hephaestus had made giant anvils from bronze and iron and fitted them on his head. But every time Typhon tried to wriggle free, there was an earthquake. And his fiery breath still erupts as lava out of Mount Etna.

The Greek god Zeus took his revenge on the monster
son of Gaia, Typhon, by hurling thunderbolts and
lightning at him. Eventually he managed to crush
him with a piece of land torn from the bottom of
Italy. The land became the island of Sicily and
Typhon was trapped under the volcano, Mount Etna.

FOUNDERS AND INVENTORS

A basket of rice from Madagascar (page 50)

Everything we use in our daily lives was invented or designed or discovered by someone. According to myths and legends, this someone could be a boy or a girl, a man or a woman, a god or a spirit. Someone was the first to light fire, find maize or eat rice. Someone was the first to invent the tools that farmers and hunters use. Someone discovered the medicines that can heal us when we are sick. Someone designed the houses we live in. Even Egypt's famous pyramids were designed by someone, a brilliant man called Imhotep.

Some myths and legends explain how cities began. It is said that Rome, for example, was founded by the twins Romulus and Remus. The name of the city, Rome (after Romulus), makes this myth seem real.

Maize discovered by the Chippewa tribe (page 51)

Romulus and Remus (pages 46-49)

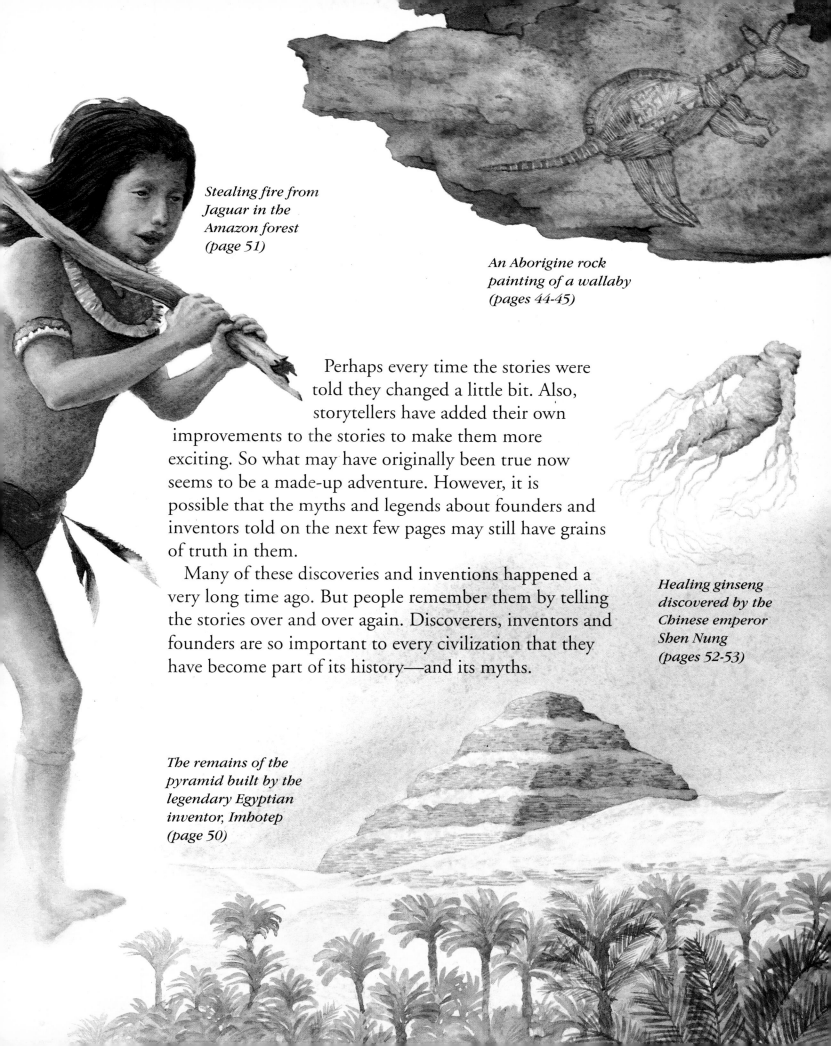

Stealing fire from Jaguar in the Amazon forest (page 51)

An Aborigine rock painting of a wallaby (pages 44-45)

Perhaps every time the stories were told they changed a little bit. Also, storytellers have added their own improvements to the stories to make them more exciting. So what may have originally been true now seems to be a made-up adventure. However, it is possible that the myths and legends about founders and inventors told on the next few pages may still have grains of truth in them.

Many of these discoveries and inventions happened a very long time ago. But people remember them by telling the stories over and over again. Discoverers, inventors and founders are so important to every civilization that they have become part of its history—and its myths.

Healing ginseng discovered by the Chinese emperor Shen Nung (pages 52-53)

The remains of the pyramid built by the legendary Egyptian inventor, Imhotep (page 50)

Myths in Daily Life
Dreamtime

Long before Europeans arrived in Australia, the Aborigines were living there. They believe that, a very long time ago, waking time and sleeping time were the same thing. Then time split and waking time and sleeping time became separate. This moment was called Alchera or Dreamtime. In the Dreamtime, the Ancestors rose from where they were sleeping under the ground and walked across the empty land. As they walked, they sang. And the things they sang about suddenly appeared: rocks, hills, trees, animals, birds and insects. The Ancestors created everything in the world—even boomerangs and spears. And the Ancestors taught the Aborigines how to live and survive. They were the founders of their world. And when they had finished their work, the Ancestors went back to sleep.

Every Australian Aborigine belongs to a clan—a large family. Every clan was founded by a particular Ancestor. Each clan is named after the thing its Ancestor created. So a person's clan name could be Honey-Ant, or Wichetty-Grub, or Flying Fox or Emu. In

the past, when they hunted for food, Aborigines were allowed to hunt for anything except the thing that their Ancestor created and after which their clan was named.

Whenever they can, the members of every clan gather together for a ceremony, or corroboree—a kind of party. They sing their Ancestor's song to make sure that the thing they are named after will be born again. If they don't sing these songs, then the thing will die and so will the clan.

At these ceremonies, the men dress up and paint their faces and bodies with colourful patterns. They act out the story of their Ancestor and draw it in the sand. The Aborigine children learn the sacred songs of their Ancestors at these ceremonies, so that they can carry on the traditions.

Every now and then Aborigines go on Walkabout. This means they walk along the paths of their Ancestors. They sing the Ancestors' songs and tell their stories to remind themselves of them.

The Aborigines' way of life is changing. They now live in cities or on mission stations or in reserves and few of them go hunting. But they still keep up their traditional customs, and they still pass on their myths.

A view of the vast open Australian landscape where the Aborigines go Walkabout. They leave painted reminders of their Ancestors on rock surfaces. The animals that live in the country are also sacred to the Aborigines.

Romulus and Remus

The story of the royal twins, born secretly and left to die, who eventually founded the great city of Rome.

In Italy, almost three thousand years ago, there was a kingdom called Alba Longa. Its king was Numitor and he ruled the land wisely and well.

But Numitor had a jealous younger brother, Amulius, who badly wanted to be king. After a fight, Amulius pulled Numitor off the throne and made himself king. But that was not enough for Amulius. Numitor had a beautiful daughter, the princess Rhea Silvia. If she had any children, they would become the rulers instead of Amulius's children. So Amulius sent Rhea Silvia to live in a temple and become a Vestal Virgin. This meant she had to promise never to marry and never to have children.

One day, Rhea Silvia went to a grove, a small group of trees, to draw water from a spring. It was the sacred grove of the god Mars. It was so peaceful there that she fell asleep. While she slept, Mars visited her. And when she woke up, she was pregnant.

Amulius found out that Rhea Silvia was going to have a baby and he was very angry. He locked her up and told his servants that when the baby was born, they were to drown it. The time came and Rhea Silvia gave birth not to one baby, but to twins. She called them Romulus and Remus.

The servants took pity on the baby boys. Instead of drowning them, they put them in a basket and floated it down the River Tiber. A few kilometres away, the basket came to rest on the river bank under a fig tree near a cave. A she-wolf found the hungry babies and carried them to the cave. There she nursed them and a woodpecker brought them insects to eat. The god Mars was quietly keeping an eye on the babies. His sacred animals, the wolf and the woodpecker, and his sacred fig tree were making sure the babies came to no harm.

Some time later, a royal shepherd, called Faustulus, was looking for some lost lambs. He peered into the cave and saw the boys with the wolf. He instantly knew who they were. Faustulus took them home and told his

Amulius's servants could not bear to kill Romulus and Remus. They placed the baby boys in a waterproof basket and sent them down the River Tiber. The boys were found on the river bank by a she-wolf. She brought them up until Faustulus found the boys and took them to his home.

wife not to tell anyone about them. He and his wife brought up the boys in secret.

Romulus and Remus grew into strong and clever young men. But sometimes they were very naughty. They would go into the fields with other boys and steal cattle. One day they went on a cattle raid and Remus was caught red-handed. He was taken by the scruff of his neck to the owner of the cattle to be punished. The owner turned out to be the old king Numitor.

Numitor questioned Remus. He asked him who his father was. "Faustulus," said Remus, because he had never known his real father. "Who else was on your raiding party?" asked Numitor. "My twin brother, Romulus," he said. Numitor began to wonder. The twins were the same age as his missing grandsons. So he asked Remus to take him to his home. There he met Romulus, and then he saw the basket the boys had been saved in. Numitor knew that he had found his grandsons.

The boys said goodbye to Faustulus and his wife and went back home with Numitor. Soon afterwards, they organized a war against the wicked Amulius. He lost the battle and Numitor was once more King of Alba Longa.

The boys grew restless living with their grandfather. When they were eighteen, they moved away from home and decided to build a city of their own. They would build it on the banks of the River Tiber, near where they had landed as babies. But the two started to argue about who would build the city. They decided to watch the sky for an omen. Remus saw six vultures fly across the sky. But Romulus saw twelve and said that this meant he should build the city.

Romulus started to dig a ditch to mark out the square shape for the city walls. Remus leaped over the ditch and shouted "Ha! What a silly little wall! How do you think that will keep your city safe?" The two boys started

The Palatine and the Aventine hills looked over the River Tiber. The brothers wanted to build their city in this area. To decide who would build the city, Romulus stood on the Palatine Hill and Remus stood on the Aventine Hill, a kilometre away. They looked to the sky for a sign. Six vultures circled over Remus and twelve vultures flew above Romulus. This showed them that Romulus should build the city.

fighting. In anger, Romulus picked up a spade and threw it at his brother. It hit Remus on the head and killed him.

Romulus was horrified. He had not meant to kill his brother. Weeping, his heart full of sorrow, he buried Remus. Then Romulus carried on building his city. When it was finished, he called it Rome. The year was said to be 753 BC.

Forty years after founding his city, Romulus disappeared in a thundercloud and was never seen again. Rome grew to be the capital city of Italy and the centre of one of the biggest empires in the world.

Discoveries

Egypt

Imhotep was a real man who lived in the 26th century BC at the court of King Zoser in ancient Egypt. He was very clever and was a brilliant architect. He was also learned in medical science and astronomy. His name has become a legend because he invented the first pyramid. This pyramid still stands today at Saqqara in Egypt. It is called the Step Pyramid because its shape builds up in a series of steps to a height of 61 metres. Before the invention of the pyramid, Egyptian kings and queens had been buried in the ground.

Later Egyptian architects copied Imhotep's design. The Egyptians were so proud of Imhotep they made him a god. They even built a temple for him, where he was worshipped. In wall paintings, Imhotep is shown as a priest with a shaved head, sitting down and reading a scroll of papyrus. His name means "he who comes in peace".

Madagascar

One day a woman and her child went to the river to wash some clothes. The child saw an insect and asked her mother what it was. The mother replied that it was a grasshopper. The child begged her to catch it. The mother managed to trap it and gave it to her child to play with. The child watched the grasshopper all day until it disappeared into the long grass. She was so upset that she cried all the way home. She cried until she became very sick. Indeed she cried herself to death. Her mother wept bitterly and her cries were heard by the Great God. So the Great God took pity on the woman and told her to bury her child in a deep marsh. A few weeks later a small plant with grains on it grew on the child's grave. The Great God told the mother to save some of the grains for sowing. The rest were to be pounded, boiled and eaten. This was the start of rice growing in Madagascar.

South America

Botoque, a Kayapo boy, went hunting for eggs in the Amazon jungle and got lost. He became frightened and hid. For days he had nothing to eat. Then Jaguar found him and took him home to give him some food. At the lair, Jaguar's wife was cooking meat over a fire. Botoque was amazed. He had never seen a fire before, because his people did not have it, nor had he eaten cooked meat. It was delicious.

But Jaguar's wife turned nasty and scratched Botoque. Terrified, he shot her with his bow and arrow and fled home with a piece of cooked meat still in his hands. His people asked him where he had found it. They went straight back to Jaguar's lair. Jaguar was not there—he was out hunting. So the villagers stole some burning coal and went home to light a fire in their village. Now the Kayapo have fire and cooked meat. Jaguar was so angry that these days he will only eat raw meat. But the image of the fire still burns in his green eyes.

North America

A Chippewa boy went into the forest. If he did not eat for a week and fought off any animals, he would prove to his people that he was a young man. One night a stranger appeared dressed in a green cloak with golden feathers in his hair. He challenged the boy to wrestle with him. Every night for three nights they fought till dawn. After the third night the stranger said that the next time the boy would kill him. Then he was to bury him and water the grave. The boy cried because he liked the stranger. But after the next battle, the stranger lay dead. The sad boy did as he was told and, in summer, he saw a green plant growing out of the grave. It rose tall and strong, with golden ears of maize. He took the maize to his people who were very happy. Maize became an important food for many peoples. The boy became a noble young man.

Shen Nung

In the Chinese Age of the Great Ten Emperors,
there was one emperor who was special. He was Shen Nung, who taught
the Chinese much about medicine and farming.

In ancient China, there was a time called the Age of the Great Ten. The Great Ten were ten emperors. Each emperor taught the Chinese people something useful. One emperor in particular became a legend because, so the legends say, he taught the Chinese some very important things.

This emperor was Shen Nung. Some legends say he had the head of an ox, but the body of a man. Because he was part ox, he invented the plough, which was pulled by an ox. He taught his subjects how to use the plough so that they could sow seed for crops. He also taught people how to farm land that was thickly overgrown with forest. If they cut down the trees in a small area and burned the stumps, they could plant their crops easily. The ash would make the soil rich, so their plants would grow well.

Shen Nung was also the god of medicine. He showed his people which plants would heal them when they were sick. The reason he became a god of medicine was that Shen Nung had a see-through stomach. He would eat strange plants and, as he ate them, he would watch what was happening inside his body. One day he gathered some leaves and stewed them in boiling water. He then drank the water. He found that this mixture cleaned

The emperor god Shen Nung pulling the plough that he invented. He taught the Chinese people how to make and use ploughs, so that they could produce their own food. If you look carefully, you can also spot his see-through stomach.

his stomach and made it feel good after he ate a meal. He had discovered the drink tea.

Another useful plant Shen Nung discovered was ginseng. He found that its roots contain substances that clean the blood of any impurities. And he found that it was a tonic—it makes tired people feel energetic, and old people feel younger.

But Shen Nung grew careless with what he ate. He swallowed a strange grass, which was so sharp that it cut his stomach into ribbons, and he died. Plants used for medicine are still very important to Chinese people. They buy them from special doctors called herbalists.

Shen Nung's wife also gave something important to Chinese society. She mastered the art of breeding silkworms. This is a skill known as sericulture. Silkworms make a thread which can then be woven into silk cloth. Chinese silk is some of the best in the world. Shen Nung's wife also became a goddess—the goddess of housecrafts.

Medicine, tea and farming—these are some of the things that made the Chinese civilization one of the greatest in the world.

Swords from the Trojan War (pages 64-67)

54

HEROES AND HEROINES

People with superhuman and noble qualities were called heroes and heroines. They may have been mortals but they were not like everyone else. Heroes were very strong, brave and wise. They risked their lives to fight against evil, save people from danger or succeed on a quest. Heroines were beautiful, like Helen of Troy, and brave, like the Tartar warrior, Gulnara.

Some heroes, such as Quetzalcoatl, King of the Aztecs, were great kings. His people were so impressed by him that after his death they worshipped him as a god. One of the earliest myths is about a great king called

Guan Di's sword (page 63)

Cuchulainn, the Celtic hero (page 63)

The Aztec plumed serpent, Quetzalcoatl (pages 56-57)

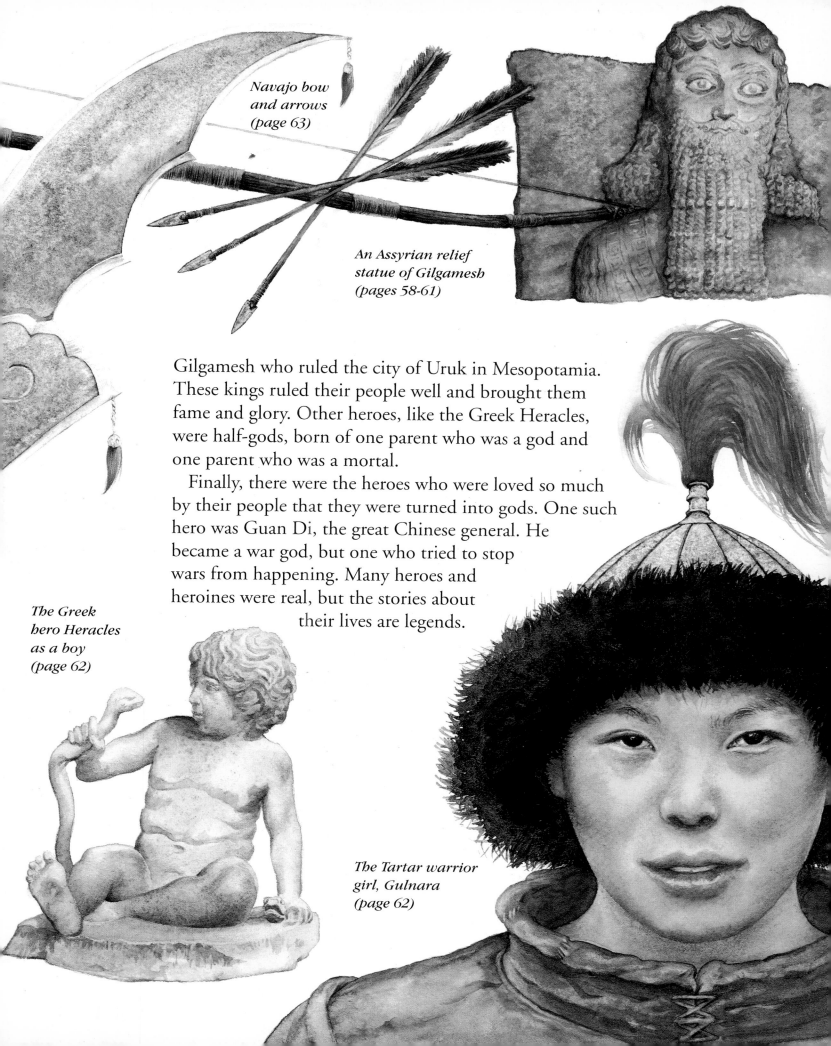

Navajo bow and arrows (page 63)

An Assyrian relief statue of Gilgamesh (pages 58-61)

Gilgamesh who ruled the city of Uruk in Mesopotamia. These kings ruled their people well and brought them fame and glory. Other heroes, like the Greek Heracles, were half-gods, born of one parent who was a god and one parent who was a mortal.

Finally, there were the heroes who were loved so much by their people that they were turned into gods. One such hero was Guan Di, the great Chinese general. He became a war god, but one who tried to stop wars from happening. Many heroes and heroines were real, but the stories about their lives are legends.

The Greek hero Heracles as a boy (page 62)

The Tartar warrior girl, Gulnara (page 62)

Myths in Daily Life
Quetzalcoatl

When Europeans were living in the Middle Ages, over seven hundred years ago, the Aztecs arrived in the land that is now known as Mexico. They were a wandering tribe who were looking for somewhere to make their home. Their gods had told them to settle in the first place where they saw an eagle with a snake in its mouth landing on a cactus. But the place where this happened was marshy and full of water. Even so, the Aztecs set to work. They drained the land and built a huge city there. They called their city Tenochtitlán. It was a beautiful place, with tall temples, canals along which people canoed, causeways (raised roads) and a market place. Over the next 200 years the Aztecs built up an empire of more than twelve million people.

One of the most powerful gods of the Aztecs was Quetzalcoatl. He was once a king and a ferocious leader, who was made a god. Aztec myths said that he was the first to bring them corn, their most important food. Quetzalcoatl was named after the quetzal, a bird with bright green and red feathers, or

The city centre that the Aztecs built in Tenochtitlán, which means "near the cactus", was the scene of great worship and sacrifice. A tall pyramid-shaped temple, dedicated to the gods of rain and war, dominated the city. The round temple nearby was dedicated to Quetzalcoatl. Human sacrifice took place at the temples.

plumes, and a long tail. Quetzalcoatl means "Plumed Serpent". He was so important that the chief priests of the city called themselves by his name. The Aztecs believed that Quetzalcoatl was also a wind god. He prophesied that high winds would cause the destruction of the world. As a result the Aztecs built him a round temple so that the wind could blow around it more easily.

The people worshipped their warlike gods all through the year. They would carry shells, pottery jars, turquoise beads and food up the steep steps of the temples to offer to the gods. The temple priests would lay these offerings on the gods' altars.

But the most important offering to the gods was people. The priests would sacrifice prisoners from the cities conquered by the Aztecs. They would cut out people's hearts and offer them to the gods. The Aztecs believed the gods would reward them for these sacrifices with rain for plentiful harvests and victories in battle. Sometimes as many as a thousand people were sacrificed a week.

In spring, the Aztecs prayed to Quetzalcoatl as the wind god to push rain clouds across the sky. They needed these clouds to water the soil so that they could plant their crops. The priests and farmers went to the mountains, where the rain gods lived. There they sacrificed children to make Quetzalcoatl bring the rain. They believed that the children's tears would make the rain fall.

The Aztec chief priests would dress as Quetzalcoatl during religious ceremonies to make themselves seem more powerful. They wore magnificent headdresses full of brightly coloured feathers, or plumes, from the quetzal bird. The priests would sacrifice people, using a knife with a stone blade.

Gilgamesh

The oldest myth we know about tells of Gilgamesh,
the King of Uruk, who
had some great adventures.

The earliest myth that we know about comes from the ancient land of Mesopotamia. A very long time ago, people carved stories into stone. The stone tablets were found, but because they were very old, they had broken into many pieces. Carefully they were joined together and this is the story they tell.

In Mesopotamia there was a young king. His name was Gilgamesh and he was the King of Uruk. He was two parts god and one part man. The god part came from his mother, who was a goddess. From her he inherited great beauty, strength and courage. But from his human father he inherited mortality—some day he was going to die.

Gilgamesh was known far and wide as a great builder of temples and cities. Of course, he did not build them himself. He got his people to do it for him. The walls and ramparts of his city Uruk were famous.

The young king was always thinking of something new to do, which meant that his subjects had to do it with him. And when he could not think of anything to do, he had to fight someone. His opponents usually lost, because he was so strong.

The people of Uruk were fed up with Gilgamesh. They were very tired from having to build walls all the time to satisfy their

energetic king. And they had lost many young men, who were killed when they fought against Gilgamesh. They prayed to the gods and pleaded with them to send someone just as strong as their king. This person could be a fighting companion for Gilgamesh and could do some of the work for them. Then they would be left in peace.

So the gods created Enkidu. He was a wild man with hair all over his body. The hair on his head grew as thick as a field of wheat. He lived in the desert with the animals. He ate grass and drank from the watering holes, just as the animals did. He was the strongest of all the wild creatures.

One day a hunter from Uruk came out into the countryside to see if his traps had caught anything. To his horror he found that the pits he had dug had been filled in by someone. And the nets he had set had been torn down. Then, when he shot a lion with an arrow, Enkidu jumped out of the long grass. In fury, the wild man threw the hunter from his chariot and carried the lion off to safety.

The hunter ran back to the city. Breathless, he told Gilgamesh that a wild man lived in the desert, who could easily be the strongest man in the world.

Gilgamesh was excited. At last someone really strong to fight with! He had to get this

The impatient king Gilgamesh stands over his people as they build the city of Uruk. The city of Uruk was a real place that was at its most prosperous around 3000 BC.

man to come to Uruk.
Gilgamesh sent a
dancing girl with a
beautiful voice to lure
Enkidu from the desert.
She walked into the desert until she
found him resting beneath a tree by a
watering hole. She stood before the watering
hole and started to dance and sing.

Enkidu stood up in amazement. He had
never seen or heard such a beautiful creature
before. And he immediately fell in love with
her. The dancing girl told him that he must
come back with her to Uruk. Enkidu was sad
to say goodbye to his animal friends in the
desert, but he had found another friend and
was glad to go with her.

When Enkidu arrived at Uruk, Gilgamesh
was waiting for him. He put up his arm so
that Enkidu could not pass by. As Enkidu
tried to push past, Gilgamesh hit him.
Enkidu then hit Gilgamesh back, so
hard that he fell down on one knee.

Then the battle really started.
Gilgamesh roared and jumped
on Enkidu. The ground
shook. Walls rattled.
Doorposts were broken. Finally,
Gilgamesh threw Enkidu to the floor and
Enkidu put up his hand to say "Enough!" He
knew that he was stronger than Gilgamesh,
but he did not want to hurt him. The two
shook hands and, from that moment on, they
became firm friends.

Enkidu stayed with Gilgamesh in his palace
for the rest of his life. And every day the
dancing girl would entertain the two by
singing and dancing for them.
Enkidu and Gilgamesh went on

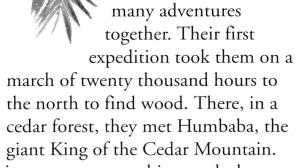

many adventures together. Their first expedition took them on a march of twenty thousand hours to the north to find wood. There, in a cedar forest, they met Humbaba, the giant King of the Cedar Mountain. His voice was a tempest, his mouth the mouth of the gods and his breath the wind. Gilgamesh called to the monster and challenged it to a fight. But Humbaba did not reply. So Gilgamesh asked the gods for help and finally managed, with much bravery, to overcome the terrible monster and kill it.

In another adventure Gilgamesh rejected the kisses of the goddess Ishtar. She was so angry that she asked her father to send a bull from heaven to kill Gilgamesh. Her father granted her wish. The bull was just about to gore Gilgamesh with its horns, when Enkidu grabbed its tail and tore it to pieces. In front of Ishtar, Enkidu skinned the beast's right leg and held it up to her saying, "If I could ever catch you, I would do the same to you." Gilgamesh then removed the bull's horns to use in sacred ceremonies.

Ishtar got her revenge by striking Enkidu with an illness. After thirteen days' struggling against the sickness, the wild man died in the arms of his friend, Gilgamesh.

Enkidu, the wild and strong man of the desert, hides from the dancing girl, daring only to peek at her through the undergrowth. He was stunned by her beauty and gracefulness. She had been sent by Gilgamesh of Uruk to find Enkidu and bring him back to the city. After watching her dance, Enkidu was easily persuaded to follow her.

Great Warriors

Greece

Some heroes fought monsters rather than wars. The greatest Greek monster-slayer was Heracles. He was half-god, half-man and superhumanly strong.

Heracles did twelve very difficult tasks, called the Twelve Labours. In one task he had to kill the Nemean Lion. Heracles's arrows just bounced off its hide. So he killed it with his bare hands, and then skinned it with its own claws. In another task, Heracles had to kill the many-headed Hydra. As soon as he struck off one head, two more sprang up. Heracles called his nephew to help him. As Heracles struck off each head, his nephew burned the stump, so that the heads could not grow back.

Russia

Gulnara, a Tartar girl, was strong and brave. She rode off to fight against the evil Khan Kuzlun. The men of the army grumbled, "What do we want with a young girl? War is for men." Gulnara ignored them. The army came to a river and on the opposite bank were Khan Kuzlun's tents. But there was no way to cross the river. That night, while everyone slept, Gulnara changed herself into a bird and spied on Kuzlun's army. As soon as dawn broke, she took the men to a hidden rope bridge and they crossed the river. When they got to Kuzlun's camp, no soldiers were there. "We'll have to tell our lord that we slew Kuzlun," said the men. But Gulnara found a camel and tied it to her. Then she scraped sand into her pouch. When they returned, the men told their story about killing Kuzlun, but Gulnara laughed at them. She hit the camel which turned into Kuzlun and shook out the sand. It was the army.

Ireland

Cuchulainn is the great hero of Irish myths. In battle, his skin turned around so that his heels and calves were at the front of his body. One eye went back into his head and became tiny, the other grew huge and red. The tip of each hair bristled with blood or a speck of light. In his last battle, against the war goddess Morrigan, Cuchulainn fought until he was so exhausted that he had to strap himself to a rock to stay upright. After his death, only Morrigan, in the form of a crow, was brave enough to touch him.

North America

The Navajos tell a story of Nayenezgani, a boy who freed the world from evil. Nayenezgani told his father, the Sun, that he wanted to save his people from monsters. So the Sun gave him magic armour, arrows made from lightning and a big stone knife. The first monster Nayenezgani fought was Yeitso. This was a giant who swallowed up a whole river every time he drank.

Nayenezgani killed the giant with the great stone knife. Then he killed a giant flesh-eating antelope. It lived on a plain where it could see far and wide. No one could get near it. So he burrowed underground until he was right under the antelope and shot it with his lightning arrow. Then he slew the giant who kicked people off mountain paths. Nayenezgani killed all the monsters, except four: Old Age, Cold, Poverty and Hunger. He left them so that people would appreciate the good things in life.

China

There once was a general in China called Guan Yu. He was nearly three metres tall, had a bright red face with a forked beard and wore a green cloak. But even though he was a general, he did not like fighting. The Chinese people were so impressed by Guan Yu's gentleness that they made him a war god and called him Guan Di. But he did not become a god who made wars. Instead, he stopped wars from happening.

The Trojan War

The great heroes of Greece and Troy fought to the death—all because a handsome prince fell in love with a beautiful married woman.

Among the greatest cities in the ancient world was Troy. Its mighty walls, which kept the people inside safe from danger, were so huge they were famous. One of the people who lived in Troy was a prince named Paris.

One day, Paris travelled to Greece to visit the Greek king Menelaus. While he was at the king's court he saw Menelaus's wife, Helen. She was the most beautiful person Paris had ever set eyes on, and in an instant he fell desperately in love with her. Paris was so in love with Helen that he asked her to come to Troy and live with him for ever. At first she would not hear of it, but after a lot of coaxing by the handsome prince she agreed, and the two eloped while Menelaus was away from home.

When Menelaus came back and found out that Helen had gone he was furious. He asked the Trojans to return his wife to him, but they refused. So he called his subjects together and told them what had happened. The Greeks were so angry that they armed themselves with weapons, called their bravest heroes together and set sail for Troy to force the Trojans to return Helen to her husband. Menelaus's brother, Agamemnon, led the army and the fleet of ships. And so the Trojan War was started.

In the dim light of dusk, when they could not be seen easily, Paris and Helen escaped from Helen's husband, and ran away to Troy. For the sake of their love, many heroes were to die in the war that then broke out between the Greeks and the Trojans.

One of the great Greek heroes who fought in the war was Achilles. He was a half-god—the son of the Greeks' most important god, Zeus. But his greatness was even more wonderful. When he was a baby, Achilles' mother dipped him in the magic waters of the Styx River. Afterwards every part of his body, except his heel, which his mother was holding as she dipped him in the river, was protected from harm by the magic of the water. To give him extra power and strength, the boy Achilles was fed on lion's meat and the marrowbone of bears. By the time he had grown up, Achilles could fight any battle almost without fear of ever being wounded.

Ajax, a giant of great courage, was another Greek hero of the war. And on the other side, fighting for the Trojans, was the warrior Hector, the noble son of the king of Troy and the younger brother of Paris.

The Greeks and Trojans fought for ten years. Both sides lost many great warriors. In one of the battles Hector was killed when Achilles pierced him through the neck with his spear. Victorious, Achilles dragged Hector's body behind his chariot three times around Troy's walls. But Achilles, too, met a most horrible end. When he was kneeling at prayer in the Temple of Apollo, the Trojan prince Paris crept in. He shot a poisoned arrow at Achilles' heel, and the great hero died. People today still talk of someone's Achilles' heel—they mean that this is his or her weak point.

The warriors continued to die, but no one seemed any closer to winning the war. In desperation, the Greeks decided to try one more trick. Some of the soldiers got back into their ships and sailed out of the harbour. The rest stayed behind. The hero Odysseus had the idea of leaving a large wooden horse for the Trojans, as a religious offering. So, out of sight of the Trojans, they built a huge wooden horse and then hid inside it.

Wearing his magical shining armour, with a breastplate made from five layers of metal, Achilles the Greek warrior fought Hector. The Trojan hero's spear bounced off Achilles' shield. Achilles then pierced Hector through the neck—where Hector had no armour—and killed the great warrior.

The Greeks' gigantic wooden horse loomed over the city gates of Troy. Inside, hidden from their sworn enemies, was an army of hot, worried Greek warriors, waiting to come out and attack the city.

When the Trojans saw the ships leaving, they flung open the city gates. People poured out of the city—they were overjoyed that the war was finally over. They danced around the city walls. Then they saw the horse and walked around it, tapping it curiously. They could not imagine what sort of strange animal this might be.

Just as they were getting suspicious, someone found a Greek soldier called Sinon hiding in the bushes nearby. They pulled him out and took the soldier prisoner, forcing him to speak. Sinon told the Trojans that if they took the wooden horse, they would win the war against the Greeks. The Trojans believed Sinon. They were delighted with the news and got their strongest men together to heave the mighty horse into the city. It was bigger than even their widest gate so they had to break open a gap in the city walls to push it through.

That night there was a great celebration in Troy, with feasts and dancing. Afterwards, while everyone was sleeping soundly, Sinon crept up to the horse and let the Greek soldiers out. Then he opened the gates and let in the Greeks who had returned in the ships during the night.

The Greeks set the city on fire and killed the Trojans with their swords. Helen was taken back home to King Menelaus. And so the Trojan War ended.

The adventures of the Trojan War are told by the Greek poet Homer in a magnificent long poem called *The Iliad*, which was composed in the eighth century BC. The poem's title comes from the Greek name for Troy, which was Ilium.

GODS
AND
SPIRITS

T he gods, goddesses and spirits in myths were imagined by people. So they took the form that people gave them in their imaginations. The chief gods and goddesses who ruled the other gods were often noble, worldly and wise. They were like the kings and queens who rule ordinary people. The Norse god Odin and his wife Frigg were dignified deities, who took special care of the famous Norse warriors. The Greek god Zeus and his wife Hera were also impressive rulers—even though they argued with each other all the time. And in Egyptian myths, the deity Osiris and his wife Isis were believed to live and rule on Earth.

A mummified cat from ancient Egypt (page 82)

A stone relief of the Phoenician god Baal (page 76)

The Inuit shaman's ceremonial mask (pages 78-79)

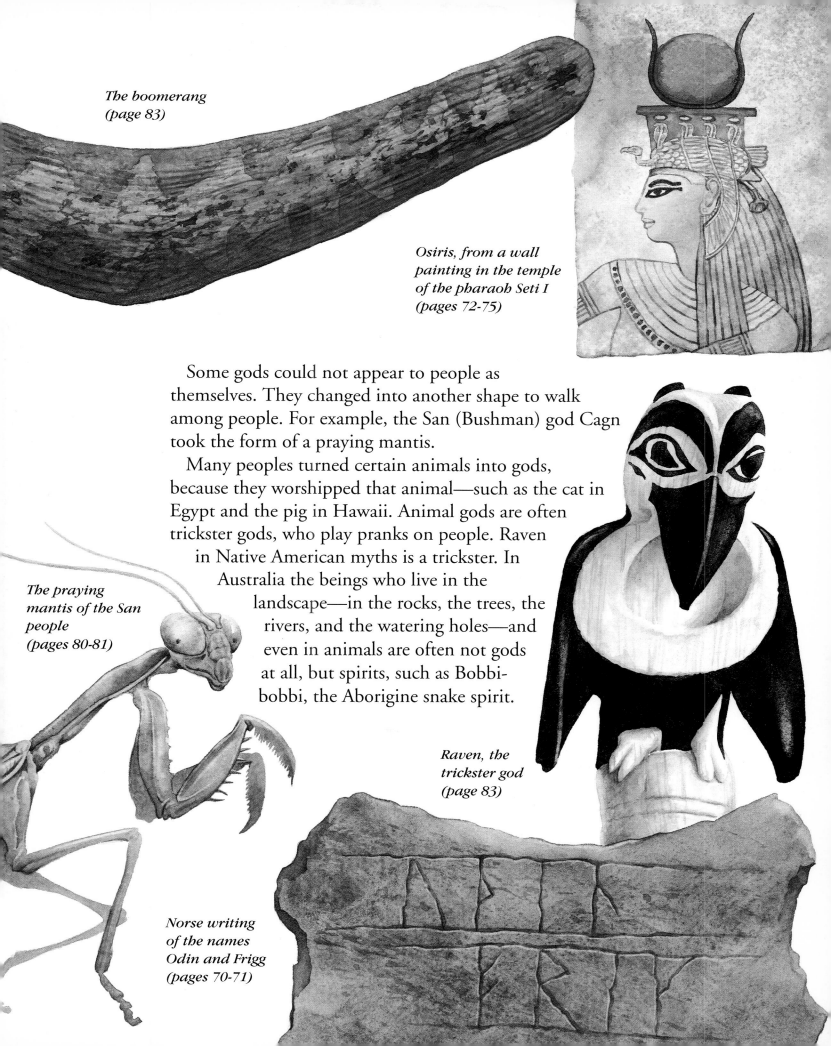

*The boomerang
(page 83)*

*Osiris, from a wall
painting in the temple
of the pharaoh Seti I
(pages 72-75)*

Some gods could not appear to people as
themselves. They changed into another shape to walk
among people. For example, the San (Bushman) god Cagn
took the form of a praying mantis.

Many peoples turned certain animals into gods,
because they worshipped that animal—such as the cat in
Egypt and the pig in Hawaii. Animal gods are often
trickster gods, who play pranks on people. Raven
in Native American myths is a trickster. In
Australia the beings who live in the
landscape—in the rocks, the trees, the
rivers, and the watering holes—and
even in animals are often not gods
at all, but spirits, such as Bobbi-
bobbi, the Aborigine snake spirit.

*The praying
mantis of the San
people
(pages 80-81)*

*Raven, the
trickster god
(page 83)*

*Norse writing
of the names
Odin and Frigg
(pages 70-71)*

Myths in Daily Life
Frigg and Odin

Before Christianity spread to Scandinavia and Iceland, the Norse peoples had their own gods and goddesses. These deities lived in a kingdom in the sky called Asgard. Ordinary people lived in Midgard on Earth. And the underworld was Niflhel, where serpents and spirits dwelled. The three worlds were joined by a giant ash tree, called Yggdrasil.

The most important deities were Odin the All-Father, his wife Frigg, and Thor the Thunder-Maker. The Norse people prayed to them outside—they did not build places of worship, such as churches or temples.

Odin, the highest god, was a god of war and knowledge. Men prayed to him before they went into battle. He was called Woden by the Teutons. These people lived south of Scandinavia, in what is now Germany, and they adopted the Norse gods, but called them by different names. From Woden's name comes the word "Wednesday". Odin had only one eye—he lost the other in return for absolute knowledge, the understanding of all things. To help him know everything, two crows sat on his shoulders, telling him all that they had ever seen and heard.

Frigg, Odin's wife, was also wise, just like Odin. She protected people's marriages and made sure that they could have children. She was tall, beautiful and like a queen.

The Norse people respected warriors a great deal. The Vikings, who were Norse people, were famous for their fierce battles. At feasts, poets and bards sang the praises of warriors. The stories of heroes were passed on by word of mouth because Norse people did not usually write things down. The only writing they had was the runes. These sticklike letters were carved into wood or stone and told the deeds of famous people.

Warriors who died went to live in Odin's court, Valhalla, or in Frigg's court, Fensalir. There they played war games and feasted, waited on by handmaids. These women were the Valkyries. They were also warriors. Odin sent them into battle and whoever saw a Valkyrie knew he was about to die. Frigg was the first of the Valkyries and was their courageous commander.

When warriors and important people died, their bodies were dressed in their finest clothes. If they were very important, they were placed in a longship and then buried. Their most precious possessions were placed beside them. Sometimes, they were laid out on a funeral pyre, which is a pile of wood where the body is burned. Then a relative would light a fire brand and set the pyre alight.

Often a slave was sacrificed and buried with the dead person, to accompany them to the other world. Food might also be buried with the dead person.

Frigg and Odin were thought of as the most perfect examples of Norse beauty and strength. To gain all knowledge, Odin had to undergo terrible adventures. His success proved that he was the bravest god.

Frigg, although married to Odin, lived in a separate house. She always carried a set of keys on her belt. Her clothes were like those worn by the richest Norse women. Her cloak was made from ermine's fur. It changed from light to dark, just as the animal's coat does in real life.

Osiris and Isis

*The Egyptian gods Osiris and Isis ruled their lands well.
However, their peace was disturbed by the greed and jealousy
of the god Seth.*

In the very early days of ancient Egypt, the god Osiris was king. He was handsome, much taller than any other man and had skin the colour of dark, polished wood. Osiris married his sister, the goddess Isis. She was tall, too, and beautiful with raven-black hair.

Osiris taught men how to make tools for farming. He showed them how to grow wheat, barley and grapes, and how to make bread, beer and wine from them. He created musical instruments and showed people how to play them. And he invented laws, built temples and taught people how to worship.

Isis was busy, too. She taught women how to grind corn and barley to make flour. She showed them how to spin flax and weave it into the finest linen. From her they also learned the arts of medicine. And she taught them the importance of marriage.

One day, Osiris decided to go and teach all these things to other people around the world. While he was gone, Isis ruled the land well. When Osiris returned, he saw that his subjects were healthy, happy, and prosperous.

But soon after Osiris came back, his brother Seth began plotting to kill him. Seth was jealous of Osiris and wanted to be king. He asked Osiris to come to dinner. At the table, Seth showed his guests a wooden chest inlaid with brass and mother-of-pearl. He said he would give it to anyone who could fit inside it. The first person he invited to climb into the chest was Osiris. As soon as Osiris was inside it, Seth and his friends quickly hammered nails into the chest to close it. Then they poured hot metal around the edges to seal it. They dragged the chest to the River Nile and threw it in.

When Osiris did not return from dinner, Isis knew that he had come to harm. She wept and wept. She cut off her long black hair, and she pulled at her clothes until she tore them into shreds. She promised that she would not rest until she had found Osiris.

Meanwhile, the chest was carried across the water to the Phoenician coast, an area now known as Lebanon. It landed at the foot of a tamarisk tree. The tree was aware that the chest contained something special. So it started to grow around the chest to protect it. Some years later, the local king, Malcandre, was building a new palace.

Even though Seth was Osiris's brother, he hated him because Osiris had all the power. When Osiris was away, Seth became accustomed to having more power. So he decided to get rid of his brother. The ancient Egyptians knew Seth as the storm god and the god of evil.

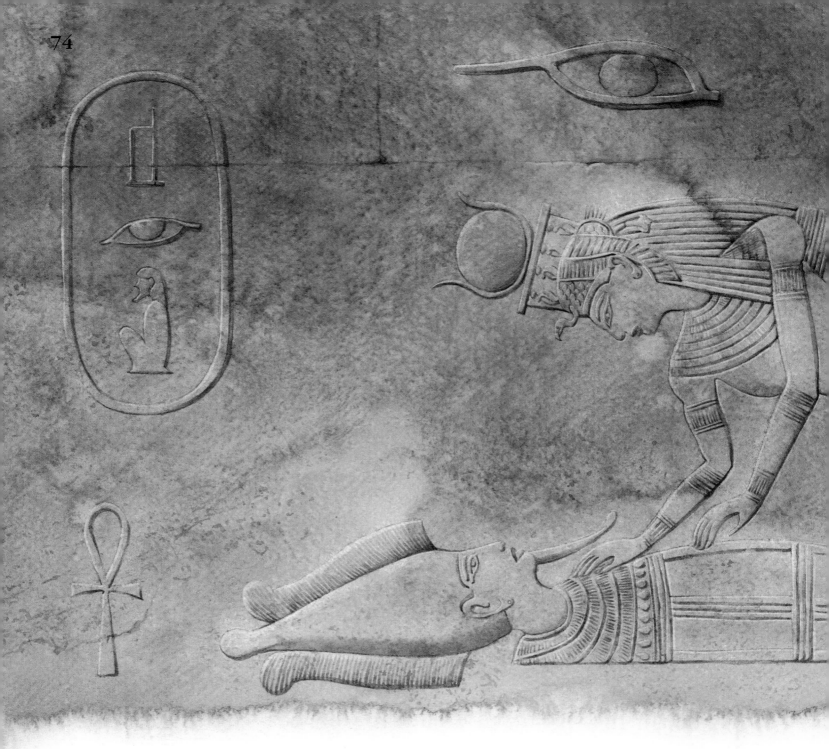

He saw the size of the tree and told his workers to cut it down to use as a column. The moment the tree was cut, it gave off such a sweet perfume that everyone started talking about it. Word of this reached Isis. She was sure the tree had something to do with Osiris, so she travelled to Phoenicia to see it. At Malcandre's court, Isis told the king why she had come. She persuaded him to have the tree chopped open. Inside the tree's trunk they found the chest. Isis brought the chest back to Egypt and hid it in the marshes. But Seth found it while he was out hunting. He was so angry that he broke open the chest with an axe, chopped Osiris's body into many little pieces, and flung them in every direction.

Isis was horrified, but she still was not defeated. Bit by bit she found all the pieces except for one, which a crab had eaten. Isis used her magic powers and her knowledge of

plants to mix up an embalming lotion (this was the first time it was used in Egypt). She rubbed it over Osiris's body to make him whole again and bring him back to life.

But Osiris told her that he would rather be ruler of the underworld, since there was no king there. Sadly, Isis had to let him go. But she was glad that, from then on, when people died, they would be governed by a good and just king in the underworld.

Isis worked to put all the pieces of Osiris's body back together again. She managed to find all of them except one, which had been eaten by a crab. Once Osiris's body was assembled, the goddess made a special ointment that she rubbed over his body. This process, known as embalming, was practised in ancient Egypt. The Egyptians did this to preserve the bodies of the dead and keep them whole, so that they might come to life again in the underworld.

Reliefs like the one above were carved on to the walls of ancient Egyptian temples and then painted. The craftsmen wanted to tell the story of Osiris and Isis to the people who worshipped at the temple.

Great Deities

Greece

Zeus was the father of the Greek gods and people. He lived on Mount Olympus with his wife Hera. She was his sister. She was also a goddess of fertility and guardian of marriage. Zeus was a fertility god, too. He was always chasing young goddesses, nymphs and mortal women, and making them pregnant. This made Hera very jealous, and the two often bickered.

Hera became so angry sometimes that she took her revenge on Zeus's children by other women. One of these children was Heracles, whose mother was Alcmena. Hera sent a pair of snakes to kill the baby in the cradle. But Heracles was so strong that he strangled them. Then, when Heracles was a man, Hera made him go mad. He killed his three sons and his wife. Zeus was so angry with Hera that he hung her upside down from heaven.

Phoenicia

Anat was a fierce Phoenician goddess and the wife of the god Baal. One day, when Baal's enemy, the god of death, Mot, was visiting the world, Baal refused to give him anything to eat. For this, Baal had to die. Mot invited him to the underworld for supper. Baal accepted, and at Mot's table he ate the food of the dead—mud. When Baal did not come home, Anat went to Mot demanding that he give her husband back but he refused. Anat set upon Mot. She cut him in half with her sickle, grilled him on a fire, ground him in a mill, and scattered him in the fields to feed the birds. By doing this, she brought her husband back to life.

Burundi

The great god in Burundi myths is called Imana. The Burundi tell a story of how Imana let Death come into the world. A very long time ago, Imana lived on Earth and people did not die. If Death appeared, Imana just chased him off with his hunting dogs.

One day, Imana was hunting a wild animal, which he knew was really Death in disguise. Imana ordered his people to go inside their houses. They all obeyed, except for one old woman. Death went up to the old lady and begged her to hide him. "Imana will be angry," she said. "Don't worry," answered Death. "After you save me, I will hide you and your family."

So she opened her mouth, and Death leaped inside her. Just then, Imana saw the old woman. "Old hag," he roared at her, "I can see you are hiding Death. From now on I will let Death kill you and all people as he wishes." Imana left the Earth and Death was allowed to spread across the world.

Tierra del Fuego

The Ona people used to live at the southern tip of South America. In Ona myths, the chief god was Temaukel. They believed that he had always existed—ever since time began. Temaukel lived above the stars where his spirit fed the universe and kept it turning. He watched over the Ona people to make sure they behaved. If they did not, he punished them with sickness and disease. The Ona people believed that when they died, their souls flew up to Temaukel. Most of the Ona died when Europeans arrived in the 19th century because they brought disease with them. There are now no Ona left.

Sedna

The great Inuit goddess of the sea, Sedna, was the child of giants and was always hungry. She now makes sure the Inuit have enough food.

In their traditional way of life, the Inuit (once called Eskimos) depend largely on the sea for their food. So it is fitting that their great goddess is a sea spirit. She is called Sedna and this is her story.

Ages and ages ago, two giants gave birth to a baby girl. But she did not stay a baby for long. She had such a huge appetite and ate so much that she quickly grew very big. She would grab any piece of meat that she saw and would gobble it up.

One night, as the giants were sleeping, they felt great pains in their legs. They woke up and saw that Sedna was trying to eat them. "We have had enough," they said. They got up, grabbed Sedna, and pulled her into their umiak (a hunting canoe). In the darkness, they started paddling out to sea. Then the giants pushed Sedna overboard into the water. But her hands rose from the waves and grabbed the side of the boat. They felt her shaking the boat and knew that if they did not do something quickly she would

overturn it and they would drown. To save themselves, the giants pulled out their knives and started cutting off Sedna's fingers. One by one the fingers fell into the sea and were swallowed up by the waves. As they sank, the fingers turned into seals, walruses, whales and shoals of fish. Sedna fell to the bottom of the ocean. There she became goddess of sea creatures.

Sedna fell to the bottom of the
ocean where she now lives. The
Inuit call on Sedna when they
cannot find any food to eat. Their
priest, known as a shaman, sends his
soul to the underworld. The soul spins
down to the heart of a whirlpool in the sea.
Then it floats into a fabulous underwater tent
where Sedna lives. The shaman's soul asks her
to send his people fish and seals for food. Then
the soul comes back to the shaman's body and
he sings about what Sedna has told him.

Cagn

The San god, Cagn, appeared as a praying mantis. In this form he enjoyed making people look like fools.

The San (who used to be called Bushmen) live in the driest parts of southern Africa. Once they lived by hunting animals and gathering roots, seeds, vegetables and honey. Their highest god, Cagn, appeared on Earth as a praying mantis. He was always playing tricks on people.

Once, Cagn decided to frighten some children. He covered himself with the skin of a hartebeest antelope and lay down on a path, pretending to be dead. Soon, some children came walking down the path, looking for wild cucumbers. They had been told never to wander far from home but they were very hungry and needed to find something to eat. When they saw the lifeless hartebeest, they leaped with joy. "It's a big fat hartebeest! We're going to have a feast," they cried.

They took out the stone knives they had in their little skin bag. The oldest boy cut off the hartebeest's front legs and shoulders. He hung them on a thornbush, so that the ants would not eat them. But the pieces lifted themselves up and moved to a tree with soft leaves. "Aah," they said, "This is much more comfortable." The boy was so scared, he would not cut off any more of the hartebeest. So the next oldest boy cut off the head. While he was doing this, a small stone fell into the hartebeest's eye. "Oh my child, be kind enough to take the stone out of my eye," said the hartebeest. In terror, the boy screamed and ran away.

Then Cagn made the hartebeest's limbs join together. The head joined itself to the neck. The shoulders stuck themselves to the body. And the skin draped itself over the flesh. The hartebeest leaped forward. It chased the children, grunting and whinnying.

The children ran home as fast as they could. Breathless, they told the elders what had happened. The elders nodded their heads wisely. "Children, you have cut up the old trickster. You cut up Cagn, the praying mantis, who was pretending to be a hartebeest." "Our hearts are burning with fear," said the children. "We are never going out alone again." And the elders just smiled and nodded to each other.

After the children had cut up the dead hartebeest, the praying mantis joined the parts together again and made it come alive. The children were terrified and started to run screaming back home. The praying mantis, inside the cut-up body of the hartebeest, followed the children, bellowing and making terrible noises. The trickster god had taught the children a good lesson: never stray too far from home.

Animal Gods

Egypt

Bastet was the daughter of Re, the sun god. Her father made her so angry one day that she changed herself into a lion. Later, while bathing in a river, her anger cooled down and she turned herself into a cat.

Bastet the cat became the goddess of music and dance. Every year, hundreds of thousands of people would come to enjoy a great festival at her temple. Parents would hang a picture of her around their children's necks to bring the children luck. When a family's cat died, the family shaved off their eyebrows in sorrow. The cat was then embalmed and wrapped in strips of cloth and became a cat mummy. Then it was buried in a cat cemetery. Mice mummies would be buried with the cat, for it to have as food on its journey to the underworld.

Hawaii

In Hawaii, a myth is told about the "hog child", Kamapua'a. This god had a pig's face and body, but hands and feet like yours and mine. He may have been ugly, but he was a very good fighter. With his snout he would dig up the ground and make huge mounds that his enemies could not climb over. And in his hands he carried a great club which could split a man's head in two with one blow. His wild snorts and grunts made his enemies run away in fear. In the past, when the Hawaiians fought many wars, they were glad to have Kamapua'a on their side.

Kamapua'a was in love with Pele, the volcano goddess. Although he was a god of war, there was a side to him that showed love.

It is not surprising that the Hawaiians had a pig god. In the past, most Hawaiians kept pigs. They were a form of wealth.

North America

The Haida, Tlingit, and Tsimshian peoples of the northwest coast of North America believe in a trickster god, named Raven. He is a wonderful creator of things. But he is also a joker and a cheat. At the beginning of time, Raven stole fresh water from Petrel to make rivers and streams on Earth. But as he flew away, Petrel lit a huge fire underneath Raven and the smoke turned Raven's white feathers black.

At first the Earth was dark. Raven thought it would be a lot easier to search for food if there was light. So he flew up into the house of the sky chief and stole a box. The box contained daylight. When Raven flew back down to Earth, he broke open the box and lit up the world. On another occasion, Raven invited a group of little people to a big meal. He told them all to sit on a mat. Then he quickly shook the mat so that the little people were flicked up into the air. They flew into the eyes of ordinary people, and became their dark pupils.

There was also a time when there were men who ran exceptionally fast. Raven did not like men being able to run so fast, so he changed them into dogs.

Australia

In northern Australia lives a group of Aborigines called the Binbinga. They tell a story about a time when their snake spirit Bobbi-bobbi lived on Earth. This was during Dreamtime, when the Ancestor spirits came to Earth and created everything on it.

Bobbi-bobbi sent some flying foxes to men for them to eat. They were not really foxes, but fruit-eating bats with faces like foxes. But the flying foxes flew too high for the men to catch. So Bobbi-bobbi pulled out one of his ribs and tossed it down to the men. "Here, use this to catch creatures that fly," he said. "You throw it in the air and it comes back to you." And so the rib became the first boomerang. But the boomerang is not only used for hunting. It also makes a very dangerous fighting weapon.

A Norse gravestone
showing Jormungandr
(page 92)

GOOD AND EVIL

The she-dragon
Tiamat attacked
by the brave god
Marduk
(page 92)

I n every mythology and in every religion, there is good and evil. The good gods and spirits fight against the evil ones. And the bad gods and spirits fight against the good ones. The tales often explain how good and bad things came into the world. And because the tales are about right and wrong, they are also one way of teaching people how to behave.

One of the earliest battles between good and evil that has been written down was between the Iranian god of goodness Ahura Mazda and the evil spirit Angra Mainyu. This story comes from Zoroastrian mythology, which was formed in the fifth century BC.

In Greek mythology, there is

A Mandan
ceremonial
shield and
spear
(page 93)

Pandora's
sealed jar of
woes
(pages 88-91)

*The buffalo demon
Mahisha
(page 93)*

no badness in the
world until the first
woman, Pandora, is created and
lets evil escape from a jar.

In most myths good wins over evil but not
in all of them. The Norse myths tell the story of
the thunder god Thor, who is killed by the
serpent demon Jormungandr when the world ends.
And in Hindu mythology, a buffalo demon Mahisha
becomes more powerful than all the Hindu gods, so they
have to create the super-goddess Durga to save them.

These battles represent what happens to us on Earth in
real life—good wins sometimes, but so
might evil. The struggle between
these two powers never ends.

*Zoroastrian
Towers of
Silence, where
the dead were
laid out
(pages 86-87)*

Myths in Daily Life
Ahura Mazda

In about 500 BC in Iran, people believed in a god called Ahura Mazda. He was the Lord of Wisdom. A prophet, whose name was Zarathustra, taught the Iranians that Ahura Mazda was the only god. He was also everything good. He was pure and truthful. He created life and gave health. He was light itself. Life on Earth was a constant fight between Ahura Mazda and the evil spirit Angra Mainyu, who created lies, death and darkness. Zarathustra said that people had to choose the only good god and live a good life. Then they would cross the bridge from this world into heaven. If they chose a life of evil, they would fall off the bridge into the abyss that was hell. Zarathustra's religion is known as Zoroastrianism.

Zarathustra's hymns, called Gathas, were written down in cuneiform. This was the only writing the Iranians had at the time. They drew on to wet clay tablets and then let them dry in the sun.

People worshipped Ahura Mazda at fire temples. Each temple had a big metal urn that stood on a stone pedestal. In the urn burned a sacred fire. The priests—known as the magi—kept the fire burning all the time. The fire was a symbol of light and purity. A person would go to the fire temple with an offering, such as sweet-scented sandalwood. And he would ask the priest to put the offering on the sacred fire and pray for him.

Every boy and girl went through a ritual ceremony to welcome them into the religion. They were given a white undershirt, known as a sudreh, and a wool cord, or a kusti, which went around their waist three times. They had to wear these all the time for the rest of their lives. The only exception was when they were washing themselves.

When a Zoroastrian died, the sudreh and kusti were laid on top of the body on a white sheet. The body was put into a Tower of Silence. These towers, which were outside the towns and cities, were open to the sky. This was so that the vultures would eat the flesh and the sun would bleach the bones white. The Zoroastrians believed that if you bury someone you pollute the ground and water; if you cremate someone you pollute the air and the fire. So this, to them, was the cleanest way to treat a dead person.

Many Iranian people followed this faith, even kings, like Darius the Great, who lived from 521 to 485 BC. This meant that the ancient Iranian kings were usually good and governed their people well.

Today, people in Iran known as Gabars still practise this religion. But most Zoroastrians live in India. They are called Parsis.

A young Zoroastrian is welcomed into the religion at the fire altar. He is wearing a white robe, or sudreh, and a cord, or kusti, is wrapped around his waist.

Pandora's Jar

According to the ancient Greeks, when the world began there was no evil. Then the god Zeus created a beautiful woman, called Pandora, and she released evil into the world.

A long time ago, so the Greek myth says, the only mortal people who lived on Earth were men. Zeus, the chief god, did not like them. But Prometheus, who had made them, did his best to protect them from Zeus.

One day, Prometheus played a trick on Zeus. At a great feast, Prometheus carved up an ox for the guests, one of whom was Zeus. He sliced the meat thinly and set it aside. Then he took a big pile of bones and covered it with fat. As the chief god, Zeus was allowed to choose his meat first. Zeus chose the largest portion he could see, which was the fat, thinking that it covered delicious morsels of meat. When he lifted off the fat and saw the bones he was very angry with Prometheus. He declared that men would never have the luxury of fire on Earth.

Undaunted, Prometheus flew off to the island of Lemnos. He knew that the smith god, Hephaestus, had his forge there, where

Prometheus travelled to the island of Lemnos and stole fire from the god Hephaestus. He did this for his precious creation, men. Hephaestus was the god of metal-working. He kept forges going all day long as he fashioned beautiful jewellery and other metal objects for the gods. Prometheus wanted to get the better of Zeus, who had decided that men were never to have the gift of fire.

he used fire to soften metal. While Hephaestus had his back turned, Prometheus quickly stole a brand of fire and carefully brought it to men.

Enraged, Zeus took his revenge on Prometheus—and men. He ordered Hephaestus to make a woman's figure from clay and water and give it a human voice. When Hephaestus had finished shaping the woman, the goddess Athena gave the figure life, taught her how to weave, and clothed her. Then the goddess Aphrodite made the woman beautiful. The Graces draped the woman with golden necklaces. The Seasons

wove a crown of spring flowers for her head. The god Hermes taught her to charm and deceive. Zeus saw her and was very pleased with the gods' work. He had created the first woman on Earth. But Zeus had formed her to be a trap.

Zeus called the woman Pandora—which means "giver of all gifts". He sent her as a present to Prometheus's brother, Epimetheus. Prometheus had warned his brother never to accept gifts from Zeus because he knew Zeus's tricks. But when Epimetheus saw Pandora he was struck by her charm and beauty. He fell hopelessly in love and he asked her to marry him. She agreed. Zeus's plan was working.

When Pandora went to live with her husband, the gods gave her a beautiful jar as a present. But the jar was sealed and they told her she was never to open it. Naturally, Pandora wondered what was in the jar. Every day she wandered through the house thinking about it. She grew more and more

curious and more and more obsessed. Finally, she could no longer contain her curiosity. Making sure that no one could see her, she tiptoed to the jar, broke the seal and slowly lifted off the lid.

Instantly, the room was filled with evil things—diseases, misfortune, sorrow, spite, malice, hatred, quarrels, worries and envy. All the evils that are in the world today flew out of that jar. Quickly, Pandora jammed the lid back on, but it was too late. Everything Prometheus had tried to protect men from, Zeus had caused to come into the world to plague it. The only thing that was left inside the jar was the spirit of hope. And this is sometimes all we have left when things are going against us.

Pandora could not contain her curiosity; she had to open the jar to find out what was inside. In opening the jar, she let out all the evil in the world. It was too late to go back on her deed. The only thing that was left in the jar was hope. Pandora slammed down the lid, so saving hope for humankind.

Battles

Mesopotamia

Some of the oldest myths we know about tell of a she-dragon, Tiamat. She lived at a time when the world was just salt water and sweet water. There was no Heaven or Earth. Tiamat created serpents, dragons and hurricanes. She was so powerful that the gods were worried. They asked the god Marduk to help. He armed himself with a bow and arrows, a huge net and a mace.

As Marduk rode his chariot across the waters toward Tiamat, she opened her great jaws to swallow him. Marduk hurled a fierce storm into her mouth so that she could not close her jaws. While she struggled, Marduk let fly an arrow into her stomach and flung his net around her. He then tore her apart with his mace and made Heaven and Earth from the pieces of her body.

Scandinavia

An evil sea serpent lay coiled around the middle of the world, according to Norse myth. Its name was Jormungandr. Every time it writhed, its many coils heaved and shook the land, creating howling tempests at sea. Thor, the thunder god, once tried to slay the serpent. But it escaped and disappeared into the depths of the ocean. Only when the world was coming to an end—a time called Ragnarok—did Thor succeed. Jormungandr was stirring up the ocean, spitting out venom over the Earth and sky. It saw Thor and, rippling its coils, moved towards him. Thor lifted his mighty hammer Mjollnir and brought it down with a heavy blow, crushing the serpent's skull. Jormungandr drew back and collapsed, fatally wounded. But Thor too was dying—he had breathed in the serpent's poison. The heroic god staggered back, but took only nine steps before he fell down dead.

North America

The Mandans of the North American grassy plains told of an evil spirit called Maninga. They feared him because this spirit wanted to kill the Mandan people. He changed himself into a flood and, like a giant tidal wave, washed through many Mandan villages.

The villagers were forced to flee from the rising waters. Their leader, Lone Man, took all the villagers to the highest village. They built a thick fence around it with the trunks of willow trees to try to stop the flood. Maninga still sent his waves after the villagers. He summoned all his strength and drew back to send a giant wave crashing over the village.

Just then, Lone Man remembered something. He recalled that Maninga loved beautiful shells with a passion. He shouted at the Mandan people to throw their best shells over the willow fence at once. Just as the gigantic wave was about to land on top of the villagers, pearly shells rained over the fence. Suddenly, the wave of water stopped and then began to retreat. Maninga let the water drain away so that he could gather the beautiful shells. Then Lone Man beat his magic drum and every last drop of the flood waters dried up—Maninga had disappeared for good.

India

The buffalo demon Mahisha was making the Hindu gods very worried. He had become so powerful that he threatened to overthrow them. He might even banish them and let evil rule the world. The gods had to do something. They decided to combine all their strength together in one super-being to fight the demon.

So they made Durga. She was a very beautiful and very fierce warrior goddess. She rode on a tiger and had ten arms. In each hand she held a weapon that the gods had given to her. Astride her tiger, Durga rode towards Mahisha. The demon turned into a raging buffalo and tried to charge her. Then he became a giant with one thousand flailing arms. Durga was not afraid. She struck him through with her lance, pierced him with her trident, and finished him off with an arrow. The gods and the world were saved.

World Maps of Myths and Legends

The myths and legends in this book come from different, widely scattered, parts of the world. The maps on these pages will help you find and remember the places in which they are told.

Each of the three round maps illustrated here shows the world from a different view. There is also a map of the world that explains how the three maps fit together.

Look at the maps to find, for example, where the Norse legends come from, or where the Inuit goddess Sedna lived.

ICELAND

Haida

Inuit

Tsimshian   CANADA

Tlingit

Chippewa

Micmac

Mandan   Onondaga

NORTH AMERICA

Navajo

ATLANTIC OCEAN

MEXICO

Aztec

Maya   CENTRAL AMERICA

GUATEMALA

PACIFIC OCEAN

Kayapo

SOUTH AMERICA

NORTH AMERICA

EUROPE

ASIA

ATLANTIC OCEAN

PACIFIC OCEAN

AFRICA

PACIFIC OCEAN

SOUTH AMERICA

INDIAN OCEAN

AUSTRALIA

Ona

TIERRA DEL FUEGO

SCANDINAVIA

Norse

IRELAND
Celtic

RUSSIA

EUROPE

Tartar

ITALY

Roman   GREECE

ASIA

SICILY
*MEDITERRANEAN
SEA*

PHOENICIA

MESOPOTAMIA

EGYPT

IRAN
Persian

AFRICA

INDIA
Hindu

SIERRA
LEONE   NIGERIA

Ibo

INDIAN
OCEAN

BURUNDI

MADAGASCAR

San

KALAHARI
DESERT
Zulu

ASIA

NORTH
AMERICA

JAPAN

CHINA

HAWAII

PACIFIC OCEAN

SULAWESI

POLYNESIA   TAHITI

INDONESIA

Aborigine

AUSTRALIA

NEW
ZEALAND

Maori

Index

Page numbers in *italic* refer to illustrations.